BE0512

1st
ptg   12—

BRAHMS

BRAHMS

Reba Paeff Mirsky

Illustrated by W. T. Mars

Follett Publishing Company Chicago   New York

Library of Congress Catalog Card Number: AC 66-16941

FIRST PRINTING

Follett Publishing Company
1010 West Washington Boulevard
Chicago, Illinois 60607

T/L 0817

To my brother,

SPINOZA PAEFF

BRAHMS

The Tenement in Bacon Alley

Rain beat against the windows of a dreary tenement building in the German city of Hamburg. The wind blew the raindrops in rhythmic spurts—one, two, three!

Inside, where the rooms were warm and full of yellow lamplight, a five-year-old boy hummed along with the storm.

> *"Rain, rain, rain!*
> *Beat upon my window pane!"*

"That's a good tune, my little Hannes," said the child's

father. Johann Jakob Brahms took up his cello and carried on a more elaborate version of the melody while the boy clapped his hands with pleasure.

"More, Papa, more! Play it on the horn now."

Laughing, the father took up another of the instruments that filled a cabinet at the side of the room. There were a violin, a viola, flute, and French horn. A great double bass leaned against the wall. "Someday you will be able to play these instruments yourself, Hannes."

"I can do it now," the boy said boldly. He seized the cello and drew the bow over the strings. A surprisingly mellow tone came forth.

"It won't be difficult to make a musician out of him," said Hannes' mother. She began setting the table with the thick, chipped dinnerware that was reserved for daily use. "But tell the boy the kind of life he has in store for him, Jakob. Make sure he knows that a musician's portion is apt to be seasoned with heartache as well as merriment."

"There is merriment enough, Christiane," Jakob said, undaunted. He beckoned smilingly to Hannes, who had not understood the undercurrent of his parents' conversation. "Come, little one. Sit here with me and I will tell you how I happened to become a musician."

"Please tell me, Papa," the boy said gravely.

"Well, I'll begin at the beginning. My father was a shopkeeper in Heide, far from here at the mouth of the Elbe River, and my parents expected me to be a shopkeeper, too. But somehow I got the idea that I must be a musician, although there were no musical instruments in the family. I had seen and heard traveling musicians and liked the sounds they made. But—ah! When I told my father I intended to be a musician, he was horrified! No! I could *not* be a musician and I had better get that foolish idea out of my head. So I ran away from home a few times, and I tried to learn music from the town piper. Finally my parents realized that I was serious about it.

"They saw that I was determined to choose my own work. Maybe it is because our name Brahms means 'brambles' that I was such a prickly boy to handle. At all events, I got my way. My parents apprenticed me to a musician, paying him a small sum so I could live with him and his family for five years in Wesselburen. I received instruction on a number of different instruments and in return I helped around the house and the garden and did whatever chores were required, like a member of the family.

"This was the only way that country boys could get a musical education. And mind you, it was not just *one* instrument we learned to play well, but several. Then, if an occasion arose where there was need for a particular musical instrument, we would be prepared to step in."

"What happened when you finished studying, Papa?"

"When I was twenty I came here to Hamburg. How exciting it was to be in a big city! I loved seeing the harbor, the big ships that came from all over the world to unload and load. I used to wander around the city walls and gates, looking at the beautiful churches and gabled houses. I prowled through the narrow winding streets, snooping among the sailors' lodging houses, the little taverns and dance halls. For a young man from the country, it was wonderfully exciting. Such sights!

Such smells! And the music. . . . Here was everything from beer-hall ballads to magnificent concerts."

"And did you play your own instruments in Hamburg, Papa?" asked Hannes.

"Whenever I could. At first I became a horn player in the band of the Town Guard. I wore a green uniform with a white embroidered collar, and on my hat there was a white pompom. At my side hung a deer knife called a *Hirschfänger*. I certainly was proud of myself in that beautiful uniform, which I wore for two years. Then I became eligible to be a citizen of Hamburg. With a few musical friends I formed a band to play on the street, passing the hat around to the listeners. Sometimes we managed to get a job in a beer garden or a dance hall. Sometimes a family hired us to play music at a birthday or wedding. At any rate, we managed to keep from starving."

"And what were you doing, Mama?" Hannes asked suddenly.

His mother tasted a pot of soup and added a bit of salt. "There is not much to tell, Hannes. I began sewing when I was thirteen. In the evenings I helped my mother. Sometimes I sewed until midnight. This went on for years. Then I worked for ten years with various families as a household servant, and after that I sewed again. When my mother died, my sister married a working man and I went to live with her. I helped in the little hardware store she ran, and earned what I could by sewing. Your father happened to take a room with us. He had only been living with us for a week when he asked me to become his wife. I could hardly believe he was serious because our ages were so different. He was only twenty-four then, and

12

I was seventeen years older."

"Your mother was an exquisite sewer and far cleverer than I. I was very lucky when she accepted me," said Jakob gallantly.

Christiane smiled gently as she limped over to the cupboard for a soup tureen. "You were born on May 7, 1833, Hannes, two years after your sister Elise."

"And then came Fritz," the boy said. The delectable smell of soup began to pervade the room. "Maybe I had better call Elise and Fritz. They are downstairs playing with Frau Becker's new kittens."

Christiane nodded, and the boy ran from the room. Within a few minutes the children rushed back. "But supper is not ready yet," the mother protested.

"Then I will play us a little dinner music to work up our appetites," Jacob said. He plucked out a booming, lively tune on the big double bass, which was twice as tall as Hannes.

"I learned to play this instrument all by myself," Jakob said proudly. "Of course, it wasn't especially difficult to do since I already knew how to play the cello as well as the other string instruments; but still there was plenty to learn. The strings are thicker and longer so that the fingers have to stretch farther. The bow is heavier, too. There were only a few musicians playing the double bass, and I thought it would be an advantage to me if a job became available in the theatre or opera orchestras where such instruments are often used. One thing you must remember, Hannes—and that is to learn to play several instruments well. Then when the chance comes, whatever the instrument required, you will be able to step in and have the job."

Hannes said loftily, "But *I* am going to play the piano. I won't need any other instruments."

"The piano!" exclaimed Jakob in surprise. "Wherever did you get such an idea? Why, we may never be able to afford such an expensive instrument. You'd better get that idea out of your head right now, my boy. I don't want to begin having trouble with you the way my parents did with me."

"What's the matter?" asked Christiane from across the room. "Has Hannes done something naughty to your instruments, Jakob?"

"No, but did you ever hear such nonsense? He says he wants to learn to play the piano! Here I have all these fine instruments, but of course he has to want something we don't possess. I guess he's going to be one of the brambly Brahmses, too."

"Don't be upset, Jakob. He's only a little boy and I'm sure he will change his mind. Try to be patient with him. Now let us eat our supper."

Jakob decided to disregard Hannes' desire to learn the piano. Until Hannes was seven, his father taught him the violin as his first instrument. He did not give up the hope that Hannes would learn to play all the instruments he himself knew. Being an all-around musician was a very good trade if you knew how to play well, were agreeable to your employer and colleagues, and not too lazy to hustle around for openings and to fill a position at short notice.

Each morning, when Jakob was unemployed, he left the three-room apartment on the second floor of the tenement

14

house on Bacon Alley. With the double bass strapped to his back like a turtle with its shell, a violin and viola in each hand, and the flute and horn in his huge pockets, he went to the hiring hall of the Musicians Union to see if a player was needed in a cafe or tavern, or at the theatre or the opera. If there was nothing, he tried again the next day. Life was precarious and money was far from plentiful. Hannes, however, continued to be unaware that his family was poor. His mother always kept the house clean and their clothes tidy and mended. And the simple food, though not abundant, was adequate.

Since their neighbors in the tenement were no better off than the Brahms family, life in Bacon Alley seemed good to Hannes. He had never been in a richer household, in the country, or among well-to-do children. If only his father would let him have piano lessons there would be nothing more to be desired.

2

Beer Halls and Piano Lessons

One morning, Hannes finished his violin lesson with his father and was praised for his good playing. "But tell me—when am I going to begin having piano lessons, Papa?"

Jakob said, "Haven't you forgotten about that yet? It costs a lot of money to go to a music teacher. If you play my instruments, I can teach you and it won't cost anything."

"But I want to play the piano, Papa. More than anything else. And I could still learn to play your instruments besides. When I earn money I'll give it all to you!"

Christiane looked at her husband pleadingly. And Jakob,

suddenly remembering his own frustrations and struggles as a child, hesitated. Then he put his hand on Hannes' shoulder and said, "Well, we'll see about it, my son. I hear that Herr Friedrich Cossel is a good piano teacher, one of the best in the city. Maybe he won't charge too much. I'll speak to him about it some day."

So later, without saying anything to Hannes, Jakob went to Cossel. He told him how musical his son was. "I think he has perfect pitch. He can tell you what note is played without looking. Could you, perhaps, take Hannes as a pupil at a price we can afford? He will be a great credit to you, I know."

"You have a piano, of course?" asked Cossel.

"I'm sorry. We haven't. But we hope to be able to afford one some day."

The teacher slapped his thigh in dismay. "How do you expect the boy to practice if you have no piano? It is impossible, Herr Brahms!"

"We'll try to find someone who will let him use theirs," said Jakob. "Just try the boy. See if he is good enough for us to think about getting a piano for him in the future."

The day and time were arranged for Hannes' first piano lesson and he went to it eagerly. It did not take long for the teacher to see that the boy did have exceptional talent and would do very well on the piano. And what a likeable lad he was! The only trouble, as Cossel saw it, was that the pale little boy wanted to compose and kept showing him the little pieces he had worked out.

Finally the teacher said, "Look here, Hannes, there's plenty of time later on for composing. At present we must spend all our time and thought on the piano studies and exercises I give you. I also was brought up on them when I studied with Herr Eduard Marxsen. I am glad to see how much you enjoy Bach's preludes and fugues, just as I did. If you get on well with your piano lessons, after a few years you may be ready to go to my own teacher, Herr Marxsen. How would you like that?"

"I would rather stay with you, Herr Cossel. I am sorry, though, that I don't have a piano at home to practice on."

"There is no reason why you can't practice on my piano when I am not using it. In that way I shall be able to hear the mistakes you make and correct you on the spot."

"Oh, thank you, Herr Cossel. My school isn't far from here. On the way home may I stop in and see if your piano is not being used?"

"Certainly, and you may practice after your lesson with me if no pupil is coming after you."

For three years Hannes studied with Cossel, practicing studies and exercises by Czerny, Cramer, and Clementi, and works of the great classical composers such as Bach, Haydn, Mozart, Beethoven, and Schubert. He made such remarkable progress that when there was to be a private subscription concert of chamber music at a cafe, with grown-up musicians, Cossel recommended that Hannes, who was only ten years old, play a solo and serve as pianist in a Beethoven quintet and in a quartet of Mozart's.

Hannes so impressed the audience with his technical ability and musicianship that a man who was an impresario, making his living by securing engagements for artists to play in Germany and in other countries, came to Hannes' father and said, "I must tell you that your son is a musical prodigy. I can easily get him a concert tour in the United States, and you and your whole family could go with him. He would make a lot of money, I am sure. Wouldn't you like that?"

Jakob was overcome at the prospect. The thought of all the wealth that Hannes' playing would bring to the impoverished family overwhelmed the poor father. He agreed at once and hastened to tell Cossel of their good fortune.

Cossel was aghast at the idea and declared, "It is out of the question, Herr Brahms! I absolutely forbid you to take the boy to America or anywhere else. He is not yet ready for such concerts and it will be bad for him in every way. I beg you to reconsider!"

Seeing that Jakob had not been persuaded to give up the idea of exploiting his son, Cossel offered to introduce Hannes to the best teacher in all of Hamburg—Herr Eduard Marxsen, his own teacher.

"I will ask him to give Hannes free lessons. They will not cost you anything," said Cossel. Jakob finally agreed to postpone his decision for awhile.

Marxsen reluctantly let Hannes play for him because he was unwilling to take on another pupil. But he was so impressed when he heard the boy that he sternly told Jakob, "Give up this idea of taking your son on a concert tour when your little plant is still so tender. I will teach him from now on for nothing."

At last Jakob agreed, his dreams of wealth collapsing.

Marxsen found that Cossel had given Hannes an excellent musical foundation; now it would be his task to develop greater independence in Hannes' left hand, teach him to transpose easily at sight from one key to another, and encourage him to compose. He took time to teach the boy theory, which is the grammar of music, and had him learn the music of earlier times, especially Bach. Of course the pupil also continued playing the compositions of Haydn, Mozart, and Beethoven.

The friendship and interest of Cossel and Marxsen meant so much to Hannes that he was devoted to them throughout his life and always tried to show his gratitude and affection for them.

When Hannes was eleven he was accepted at Herr Hoffmann's private school on a scholarship. It was a much better school and nearer home than the one he had gone to before, and there he learned a little Latin, French, English, mathematics, and natural history. Knowing that his school years were numbered, since his help in supplementing the family income would be needed as soon as possible, he made the most of his four years there.

Since Hannes was already such a good pianist, Jakob was able to get him night jobs playing at various Hamburg dance halls, taverns, or restaurants, even though he was only thirteen. Before long the tavern owners were so impressed by Hannes' ability to play in a lively way that he was rarely without work. The pay was small, to be sure; but they told him he could have as much to drink as he wished. Luckily Hannes did not take advantage of this offer. When he was older and spoke of his early life, he said he could easily have become a drunkard under these conditions.

To his parents it did not seem too early for Hannes to be

bringing in money, because they themselves had had to work just as early to help their families. Christiane could see no harm in his being in such a rough environment; she probably felt that since he came from a good home where he was taught honesty and the need for good character and morals, such influences would counteract anything bad.

Playing night after night in the bars and dance halls, in an atmosphere filled with beer fumes and tobacco smoke, Hannes, with his excellent memory, soon knew all the dance tunes by heart. To while away the time he played endless variations on them, and he also kept on the music rack of the piano a book of poetry. This he would read as his nimble fingers played mechanically, stimulating the sailors to dance and sing. Hannes' love of books, like his knowledge of music, was increasing all the time.

But Hannes would come home tired. He said nothing to his mother about the coarse talk and low behavior of the sailors and their girls. During the day, he practised his lessons for Marxsen in every spare moment, composed pieces for the teacher to criticise, and did his schoolwork. Marxsen decided there was no use telling the parents that it was bad for their son's health to play night after night in the places he did, for the family was in desperate need of money. But soon Jakob himself noticed how pale and nervous Hannes was and he realized he might become ill.

From time to time Hannes' father had a job playing the double bass with a small group at a restaurant called the Alster Pavilion, near the Hamburg docks. There he became acquainted with one of the patrons, Adolf Giesemann, the owner of a paper mill and small farm in Winsen, about twenty miles from Hamburg. Because Giesemann enjoyed the good food and music at the Alster Pavilion, he often went there while in the city on business. He had become acquainted with Jakob, who was very sociable and liked to talk about his remarkable young Johannes to any patron who would listen to him. Giesemann became interested in Jakob's talented son.

One day when Giesemann came in and asked after Hannes, Jakob told him, "To tell the truth, I am worried about my son's health. He works very hard and, as you know, the Hamburg air is none too healthy. At the moment he has no job. I was wondering if perhaps he could spend a few weeks with you and your family in the country. It would do him such a world of good to be in the fresh air! He is a good musician, and in return he could give your daughter piano lessons. I believe you told me she is about Hannes' age."

"It would be a pleasure to have him," the kindly businessman said. "I expect to return to Hamburg very soon, and I will gladly take him back with me to Winsen." And this he did.

When Hannes for the first time saw the woods, smelled the fragrant flowers, gazed at the trees and streams, and heard the singing birds and the lambs bleating, he was enraptured. The good Giesemann family and their neighbors immediately took him to their hearts, especially when they saw what a capable and talented musician he was. A group of twelve young men—school teachers, shopkeepers, and clerks—had formed a small choral group which met once a week. Hearing how well Hannes played, they asked him, despite his youth, if he would be their choir conductor. The boy was delighted.

They rehearsed late on Saturdays at someone's house, or on Sunday evenings at some cafe where Giesemann, his family and friends would listen to Hannes playing gay waltzes for dancing and solos as well. Hannes transposed and arranged many German folk songs for the group to sing in four parts, and wrote a few choral compositions, one of them to the letters of the alphabet and another called "The Postilion's Morning Song."

Hannes blossomed in this happy, healthy atmosphere. He ate well and slept soundly in the fresh country air; he had books to read, and from a lending library in the village he obtained stories of adventure which he and Lieschen Giesemann enjoyed together. The story "The Beautiful Magelone and Knight Peter with the Silver Keys" was one of their favorites. Later Hannes based one of his famous song cycles on these tales. He went on walks with Lieschen in the forest, swam in the river, practiced and composed. Every Wednesday he returned by steamboat to Hamburg for his piano lesson with Marxsen, and stayed overnight with his family in their new home. Sometimes Lieschen came with him and then shared a small bedroom with his sister Elise. Lieschen was particularly fond of Hannes' mother, and when she was with the Brahmses she cheerfully fetched water from the pump down in the alleyway.

She found Hannes' home very small and dark, but neat and clean. It was in a better neighborhood now, at Damthorwall. In the parlor where the secondhand upright piano stood there was only one small window which looked out on a squalid courtyard. Sometimes when she came from Winsen she would bring a few cheerful plants to set in the windows, hoping they would brighten the dark little rooms; but because of lack of sun and clean air the plants did not do well and withered. Lieschen saw the little shelf with Hannes' treasured books, and realized that the most welcome gift anyone could give him was a book, especially if it contained tales of knights and their tournaments.

Never had Hannes known such happy days as in Winsen. When he returned home in the autumn he was so much healthier and sturdier, his thin face now filled out and rosy, that Christiane overflowed with thankfulness for the miracle the Giesemanns had accomplished.

When Hannes was fifteen, Marxsen thought his pupil was ready to give his first public concert. So in September, 1848, Hannes gave a benefit concert with a violinist. On the program were pieces that showed off his technical ability, and in addition he played one of his favorite fugues by Bach, who was at that time a strange and unfamiliar composer to most audiences. Hannes was singled out by the music critic of the Hamburg newspaper who said, "Young Brahms showed great facility, precision, power, and certainty; but he caused great surprise and obtained unanimous applause by the intelligence of his interpretation."

He continued playing in the evening at bars and dance halls, and in the daytime he went to school. He could hardly wait for spring to come so he could go back to the Giesemanns'; it was a second home for him. The choral society was delighted to see their young conductor back, and he soon arranged more folk songs for them.

One day when he was to go to Hamburg for his piano lesson and Lieschen was to accompany him, she persuaded her father to treat them to two tickets for the Hamburg Opera's performance of Mozart's *Marriage of Figaro*. Hannes had never been to an opera before and he was beside himself with excitement when he heard the wonderful and inspiring music. Never in his life would he forget it.

"What a genius Mozart was!" exclaimed Lieschen.

"And just think," added Hannes, "he was already writing music when he was only five years old, and giving concerts all over Europe soon after that. What a pity he died so young, at thirty-five! Think how much glorious music he might have written in later years."

When Hannes returned to Hamburg at the end of the summer his school education was finished and he was now expected to make his own way. He was considered a professional musician at fifteen, and as such would have to contribute regularly to the support of the family and to the education of his thirteen-year-old brother Fritz, who was also going to be a musician and pianist. As a parting present to Lieschen, Hannes copied out for her the four-part songs he had composed and dedicated to the Winsen Choral Society.

There had been a solemn farewell ceremony at the last meeting of the choral group. The master-baker, a strong man, had lifted Hannes on his shoulders and marched around the table several times with him, followed by the singing members of the choral society. It was warming to know that whenever he returned to Winsen he would find an enthusiastic welcome from these wonderful friends.

Hannes' father was now the double bass player in the Hamburg Philharmonic Orchestra. One day in February, 1848, he returned home from a rehearsal to announce to Hannes that the great Hungarian violinist Josef Joachim, who at seventeen was only two years older than Hannes, was to be in Hamburg in a few weeks to give a concert with his orchestra.

Hannes saved up his money and bought the cheapest ticket. Not being able to afford to buy the program and having heard his father say that Joachim was going to play some of his own compositions, Hannes thought that one marvelous violin concerto he heard was by Joachim. When Hannes told Marxsen how magnificent Joachim's concerto was, Marxsen agreed. "Of course it was magnificent. It was by Beethoven!"

Hannes now began giving piano lessons for a modest fee as well as playing in the taverns at night. And he was glad when a Hamburg music publisher hired him to make arrangements of popular light music under the pseudonym of G. W. Marks.

Young Brahms did not wish to be remembered for arranging marches and dance music for cafe orchestras. However, whatever he earned was highly welcome and needed at home. Sometimes he accompanied singers who were not particularly talented; now and then he got a concert engagement or played at a private party.

For one of his programs he played the "Waldstein Sonata" of Beethoven and a composition of his own, a fantasy on a popular waltz. Because of his experience in playing dance music at the taverns, Hannes had become unusually skillful at this kind of composition. His ability to make variations was already so marked that he amazed everyone who heard him. Variations, where a theme is given out simply and then repeated many times with changes that do not hide its identity, are a little like a dinner served up in many courses with different types of cooking and sauces. Although his talent as a pianist was increasing all the time, Marxsen did not yet consider him to be in the class of the virtuoso pianists who came to perform in Hamburg. Anyway, as far as Hannes was concerned it was not as a pianist that he hoped to become known but as a composer.

He was already showing much power and inventiveness in his compositions, such as his "Scherzo in E♭" and the "Piano Sonata in F♯ Minor," his first known original music. He set music to the words of poetry he enjoyed and tried his hand at another trio and a string quartet. In addition to his studies with Marxsen, he read books on the theory of music and studied the works of old masters in order to improve his compositions. There was so much to learn!

Having few friends, Hannes turned chiefly to his mother, whose affection and understanding he was always able to count on. She liked to hear about the books he was reading, for she had always enjoyed books, too. When he was little she had read aloud to him, and would recite long poems, especially those by Schiller. She knew the Bible well and could repeat many of the passages from memory.

Although Hannes loved his father as well, he could not discuss his intimate thoughts with him as easily as he could with his mother. And somehow he never felt he had much in common with his sister Elise and brother Fritz. Elise always seemed to be having headaches, and Fritz, studying music, too, was often unpleasant and envious of Hannes' ability. Later on, life became even more bitter for Fritz when he was a piano teacher in Hamburg and was referred to as "the wrong Brahms."

Since Hannes' home was small and crowded, and his piano inadequate, he sometimes practised at the piano firm of Baumgarten and Heinz, who were glad to let him come there and use one of their fine pianos whenever he wished. There he met a musical young woman, Louise Japha, seven years older than himself. She often spoke to him about the composer Robert Schumann and his wife Clara, an outstanding pianist. She told Hannes how much she wished to go to Düsseldorf and study piano and composition with them.

Hannes and Louise often played duets and showed each other their compositions; it was in answer to her question on how he composed a song that he said: "I generally read a poem through very slowly and then, as a rule, I find that the melody is there."

Due to her urging he decided to leave a package of his compositions at the hotel in Hamburg where the Schumanns were staying during a concert tour, hoping to have Robert Schumann's opinion of them. To his dismay, he received the package back unopened after many days. Hannes was terribly hurt and disappointed by this; his mother's argument that Schumann was no doubt too busy to take the time to look over his compositions left him unconvinced.

In these days Hannes was often discouraged; he felt he was getting nowhere, becoming only a humdrum musician who gave piano lessons, played dull accompaniments and wrote trivial pieces under a pseudonym for any publisher who asked him. What could all this lead to?

Jakob, too, was beginning to show his disillusionment about Hannes' future. He had expected his young musical prodigy to bring honor and wealth to the family by this time; but what had come of their expectations? So far, nothing. He told Christiane, "I think it's time that our Hannes got away from Hamburg where he is hardly appreciated. Perhaps he would show his worth better elsewhere."

"Perhaps so, Jakob. I have noticed that Hannes is not very happy here. I am sure that if an opportunity were offered him to go to some other place he would gladly accept it. He has often told me how much he longs to see the world."

At last, when Hannes was almost twenty, an opportunity presented itself. The young Hungarian violinist, Eduard Reményi, three years older than Hannes, who played gypsy music in a spectacularly brilliant way and who was to influence some of Hannes' later compositions, came to give a concert in Hamburg. He was not the outstanding musician and violin virtuoso that Josef Joachim was, but he was such a great showman that the audiences were carried away and entranced by his wild Hungarian gypsy music.

Reményi got acquainted with Hannes Brahms at a party given in his honor in the home of a rich Hamburg merchant. Having heard how beautifully Brahms played, Reményi invited him to come along on a concert tour he planned. They left a few months before Hannes' twentieth birthday. At that same time, Louise Japha left for Düsseldorf to study with the Schumanns.

Brahms took along some of his own compositions: part of a piano concerto, a sonata for violin and piano, a string quartet and some songs—in case someone might be interested in hearing them.

Jakob sighed with relief. "Now, dear Christiane, we'll see what our Hannes amounts to. It was high time for him to leave the nest and be on his own."

Although Christiane was glad for her son to have this opportunity, she was sad to see her beloved boy go away to distant places. How she would worry about his health and safety! Such dreadful things could happen!

❦ { 3 } ❧

Adventures of a Young Pianist

Never having been further away from Hamburg than Winsen, young Johannes Brahms was thrilled to be Reményi's accompanist and to be allowed to play occasional solos. Reményi had pointed out the advantages of their giving a joint program: in this way Brahms might begin to earn a reputation for himself as a concert pianist. And furthermore, Reményi said that he planned for them to go to Hanover later on, where he would introduce Brahms to Joachim, whom he had known in Hungary and who was now the concert master of the King of

32

Hanover's court orchestra. Recalling how impressed he was by Joachim when he first heard him in Hamburg, Brahms was delighted at the prospect.

Hardly had they started out on the concert tour when Brahms realized that Reményi was going to be extremely difficult to get along with. He was so temperamental, so full of himself, and so anxious for the public to notice only him that he resented it when Brahms played his solos and received much applause. Once, however, Reményi did show an unexpected generosity.

It often happened that when they played in small towns, they found the concert piano out of tune. Usually Reményi could tune his violin to adjust to it. However in Celle, the piano was a half tone lower than it should have been and there was no tuner available. Reményi refused to tune down his strings to that degree. Therefore it was necessary either to cancel the concert or for Brahms to transpose everything on the program up a half tone, and all from memory, too. This was no small achievement; but having had such excellent training with Marxsen in transposition, Brahms was able to play through the whole program perfectly, including a difficult and beautiful Beethoven sonata, in a different key from the original. Even Reményi was so impressed that at the end of the program he announced to the audience what Brahms had done. They applauded him heartily. This time Reményi did not begrudge the acclaim.

Among the many places where they played was Winsen. The Giesemanns, who looked upon Brahms as their child, were delighted to have him and Reményi stay with them and could not do enough to show their pleasure. The school teachers and shopkeepers from the choir visited Brahms, all showing their warm friendship and affection. They were proud of him and felt he was justifying the great musical promise he had shown as a boy. They had no doubt he would go far.

Finally, after concerts in Lüneburg and Hildesheim, Brahms and Reményi arrived in Hanover, the furthest away from home that Brahms had ever been. Joachim, who was twenty-two, was immediately struck by the great contrast between his two visitors. Reményi was dark and excitable, a showoff; Brahms, three years younger, with long fair hair and deep blue eyes, was modest and somewhat shy. While Reményi boasted about his success in the various places they had played, Brahms remained quiet and reserved, embarrassed by his immodest companion. Observing Brahms quietly, Joachim realized immediately what a splendid person he was. Joachim was attracted by the young pianist's thoughtful face and decided he wanted to know him better, not only as a musician but as a friend.

When Joachim managed to escape from Reményi's chatter and have a conversation alone with Brahms, he found him at first a rather untalkative person. But soon Brahms felt at ease with the kindly Joachim and began pouring out his thoughts, telling him all about his compositions and hopes as a composer. Joachim then asked him to play some of his work. When Brahms finished playing, Joachim was so excited by the beauty and originality of his music and by the magnificent way he played the piano that he could not help wondering, "Where has this very talented young man been concealing himself all this time?"

Hanover was a small state ruled by its own Grand Duke. Germany at that time was not unified but consisted of about one hundred separate duchies, each with its own luxurious court. Many of the rulers kept their own orchestras and opera singers. The Hanover court was especially well known for its excellent music, and its Grand Duke was also called the King of Hanover.

Although Reményi and Brahms spent only a few days in Hanover, it was long enough for Brahms and Joachim to become fast friends. For the first time Brahms found someone who understood him and his music, someone with whom he could talk freely about his dreams as a composer. Joachim wrote at the time to a friend:

> *Brahms has a wonderful talent for composing and a talent which can develop to its fullest bloom only in perfect seclusion—pure as a diamond, soft as snow. His playing shows that intensive spark, that energy and rhythmic precision which prophesy the artist; and his compositions already contain more significance than I have ever encountered in any music student of this age.*

As soon as Joachim learned that Reményi wished to go to Weimar to visit the famous Hungarian composer and pianist Franz Liszt, whom Joachim knew well, he wrote a letter of introduction. Brahms was very eager to meet Liszt and hear his compositions. Excitedly he set forth with Reményi for Weimar, where Liszt had been the conductor of the court opera house and court theatre since 1848.

Before parting, Joachim took Brahms aside and said, "If for any reason you should part company with Reményi"—and somehow he felt the time would soon come—"be sure to visit me in Göttingen during the summer. I am planning to attend some lectures at the university there. I want very much to see you again."

At Weimar Reményi and Brahms were received cordially by Liszt, whose long straight hair fell to his shoulders. After reading Joachim's enthusiastic letter of introduction about the two young men Liszt was especially gracious to them. Liszt, forty-two years old and surrounded by fanatically admiring students and sycophants, obviously enjoyed the adulation. Brahms was disappointed to discover that Liszt was almost as much of a flamboyant showman as Reményi! He found it distasteful to observe how much Liszt enjoyed the praise, attention, and luxury of his surroundings.

Liszt played some of his own compositions, but Brahms found them superficial and showy. Brahms respected him as a brilliant pianist, but he found Liszt's overdramatic music disappointing. Reményi had been telling Hannes before they came to Weimar what a splendid composer Liszt was, and Brahms had been expecting a memorable experience.

After playing his own works, Liszt turned to Brahms, who was standing with his eyes closed against a tapestried wall, and said, "Brahms, I understand you are a composer too. Won't you play something of your own for us?"

Very ill at ease and uncomfortable in such a gathering of sophisticated people, and with mixed feelings about Liszt, Brahms could not be induced either to play or to show his compositions. He had put them on a table when he entered the room; and now Liszt picked up the roll of manuscripts and said, "Well, if you won't play them for us, I shall have to do it myself."

He played Brahms's "Scherzo in E♭ Minor" with such remarkable spirit and power that Brahms was overcome. What a stupendous pianist Liszt was! If only Liszt had played works by Bach, Mozart, and Beethoven instead of lesser music, Brahms would have worshipped him. But Brahms found the music of Liszt and Wagner unpleasant. It was considered to be very modern, and composers belonging to the New German School of music refused to be hampered by the tradition of classical music. Brahms later told a friend, "I saw that I did not belong there at Weimar. I should have had to lie about my tastes, and that I could never do."

The relationship between Brahms and Reményi grew cooler and cooler, and soon after reaching Weimar, Reményi suggested that Brahms now try his luck alone. Brahms did not know how he would be able to make ends meet, but what he did know was that he would go at once to visit Joachim in Göttingen. He wrote to tell him he was coming:

June 29, 1853

Dear Herr Joachim:

Reményi is leaving Weimar without me. It is his own wish, for my manner could not have given him the slightest

pretext for doing so. . . . I cannot return to Hamburg with
nothing to show, although there I should feel most happy
with my heart tuned in C–G♯. I must at least see two or three
of my compositions in print, so that I can look my parents
in the face.

Will you write to me soon, if you are going to be at
Göttingen in the next few days? This would make me ex-
tremely happy; and may I visit you there? I am presump-
tuous, but my position and my dejection force me to be.

Joachim was delighted to have him come, and when
Brahms arrived they spent many happy weeks together making music, reading, walking, having discussions about the
philosophy lectures Joachim was attending, admiring each
other's talent and reveling in the merry company of other
students.

When Brahms's parents learned that the brilliant tour they
had imagined with Reményi had come to an end, and that their
son was going to Göttingen to stay with Joachim for a holiday,
they were shocked. Christiane, who always did the letter-writ-
ing, wrote:

You have not written plainly enough about what is hap-
pening. For example, you say you need no money. But even
if you have free lodging, food and drink, you must have clean
linen, your boots will wear out, and after all, how can one
live without money? If you have to beg every little thing from
Joachim, you will be under too great an obligation to the
gentleman. You had better write to Herr Marxsen. He will

advise you what to do. But you must write the exact truth, otherwise the same thing will happen as with Reményi. You understand people too little and trust them too much.

Brahms, upset by the letter, showed it to Joachim. "Don't worry about it," said Joachim. "I'll write to reassure your parents, and then they'll feel easier about your being here."

On July 25, 1853, Joachim wrote:

Allow me, although I am a stranger to you, to write and tell you how fortunate I feel in the companionship of your Johannes. For who better than his parents can know the joy which their son can give? Your Johannes has stimulated my work as an artist to an extent beyond my hopes. To work with him toward a mutual goal is a spur for me on the thorny path that we musicians have to walk through life. His purity, his independence (young though he is) and the singular wealth of his heart and mind find sympathetic expression in his music, just as his whole nature will bring joy to all those who come into spiritual contact with him. How wonderful it will be when his artistic powers are revealed in a work accessible to everyone.

You will understand my wish to have him near me as long as his presence does not interfere with his duty to himself. I believe, moreover, that Johannes, too, finds it pleasant to live in quiet Göttingen, where he is sure to find in the music director and myself two men who are glad to follow his little idiosyncrasies in life and art.

How glad I should be if I could render my friend

39

Johannes a genuine service; for it goes without saying that
my friendship is always at his disposal. I can only hope that
our new bond will find the blessing of your approval.

Truly yours,
Josef Joachim

Jakob and Christiane were so proud of the letter from the famous violinist that they showed it to all their friends, among them the Giesemann family.

While at Göttingen Joachim suggested that he and Brahms give a concert together; thus Brahms would earn a little money, for he wished to visit western Germany and make a journey on foot along the Rhine. The concert was successful and when Brahms left, Joachim gave him letters of introduction to friends along his way; there was also a letter to Robert and Clara Schumann, whom Joachim urged Brahms to visit despite the latter's wounded pride. Joachim could not sufficiently praise the Schumanns as musicians and delightful people, but Brahms would not promise to visit them.

The beauty of the countryside along the Rhine filled Brahms with the greatest happiness. He wrote to his parents about the wonderful walking tour he was taking and described the splendid overhanging rocks and the great river.

His mother, always apprehensive about his safety, wrote:

It is a lovely trip you are making, but surely it must some-
times be very dangerous. Such steep rocks! How easily you
could fall there! I tremble when I think of it. And you are
strong, of course, but one can overdo things with too much

climbing . . . so please take care of yourself, and for heaven's sake don't go out in a thunderstorm!

When Brahms was in Bonn he went to visit a friend of Joachim's, who in turn introduced him to other musical people. At the home of Herr Deichmann he was shown some of Schumann's compositions which he had never seen or heard before. After poring over them he was so delighted and charmed by the freshness of the music that he forgot his former feeling of chagrin about Schumann and decided that he must by all means visit him in Düsseldorf.

Schumann had already had a letter from Joachim. Consequently when Brahms appeared at the door, he received a hearty welcome. In Schumann's home there was none of the luxury and aristocratic atmosphere that had made Brahms feel so emotionally frozen in Liszt's house, nor were there the over-admiring and fawning pupils. Here there were books, music, plants, and flowers to make it homelike and welcoming.

Schumann asked Brahms to play him some of his compositions; so he began with his recently finished "Piano Sonata in C Major" and was going to continue with the one in F♯ minor, the "E♭ Minor Scherzo" and several songs. Hardly had Brahms finished the first piece when Schumann jumped up. "Just a moment, please! I want my wife to hear you."

He went to get his wife Clara, who was at that time thirty-four years old and a remarkable pianist. She was an attractive woman with thick brown hair parted in the middle and braided into a knot in back. Her husband said, "Now you shall hear such music, dear Clara, as you have never heard. Young man, begin the piece again!"

Later on, Schumann said privately to Clara, "There is nothing more to teach this boy. He is a finished musician. He is one of the handsomest and most talented youths I have ever met."

With these kind and simple Schumanns, Brahms's usual restraint disappeared and he was able to play with all the happiness and artistry that was natural to him. Schumann was so excited at the discovery of this unknown talent that he was beside himself. Both he and Clara kept independent diaries, making daily entries of their activities and thoughts. Clara wrote enthusiastically about their impressions of Brahms:

> *How moving it is to observe this young man at the piano, with his remarkable face transfigured, his slender hands surmounting with ease the greatest technical difficulties (for his compositions are very hard to play). He has studied with Marxsen in Hamburg, but what he plays for us is so accomplished that one would think the dear God had sent him into the world a finished artist. A magnificent future awaits him, for once he starts composing for orchestra his imagination will find its full scope. . . .*

The Schumanns invited Brahms to have his meals with them every day while he was in Düsseldorf, so they might play for each other and so that Brahms could enjoy their seven children, whose ages ranged from two to twelve years old. With children Brahms was never shy, and he immediately became a favorite with Schumann's little ones. The friendship between the young man of twenty and Robert Schumann, then forty-three, was beautiful to see. Schumann had been conductor of the municipal orchestra at Düsseldorf, but his chief pleasure was in composing and in showing his warm interest in the young musicians who were his disciples. Joachim was among them and had told Brahms that Schumann was the living representative of the kind of music he loved.

Brahms was ashamed of himself for having misjudged such a splendid person as Robert Schumann. What an idiot he had been not to want to meet this wonderful family!

❧{4}❧

The Young Eagle

Because of the Schumanns' encouragement and their warm friendship, Brahms flourished like a plant that had been thirsting for water. Their deep interest brought out the best in him; with them he felt less shy and reserved, talking as easily to Clara and Robert as if he were part of their family.

It was a joy to be in the Schumanns' cultured musical household. While he was in Düsseldorf he looked up Louise Japha and her sister, who had come to study with the Schumanns. Brahms told them all about his tour with Reményi, about his visits to Hanover, Weimar, and Göttingen, and his hike along the Rhine. Louise inquired about his parents, and Brahms showed them letters from his mother and said, "I get one like this every week. My dear mother keeps her promise. When she has no news, she copies things from newspapers to entertain me!"

Clara and Robert Schumann introduced "the Young Eagle," as they called Brahms, to all their musical friends as if he were their most precious possession. There were musical evenings, for Schumann's greatest wish was to help make Brahms known, to get his music published and heard. Schumann wrote to his own music publisher, Breitkopf & Härtel in Leipzig, recommending that they publish Brahms's imaginative compositions:

> *A young man here has deeply impressed us with his splendid music. I am convinced he will be a sensation in the musical world.*

Schumann then advised Brahms to go to Leipzig for a week to play his works for the publishers, because they would then get a better idea of how his music sounded. "Your beautiful playing is an essential part of your music," Schumann said. "I do not remember having heard such original tone effects before."

Schumann also sent to a music magazine for publication a long and enthusiastic article about Brahms and his tremendous ability as a composer. Schumann declared that a new genius had appeared on the horizon and that a great career lay ahead of Brahms.

> . . . *He is here, a youth over whose cradle Graces and Titans stood guard. His name is Johannes Brahms, and he comes from Hamburg where he has been working in obscurity, trained in his art by an excellent teacher [Marxsen] who sends me enthusiastic reports of him; recommended to me recently by a well-known and respected master [Joachim]. Even outwardly, he carried on his person all the marks of a chosen man. Seated at the piano, he introduced us to wondrous regions. We were drawn into a circle whose magic continually grew on us. To this was added an altogether inspired style of playing which transformed the piano into an orchestra of lamenting and exultant voices. There were sonatas—veiled symphonies, rather; and songs whose poetry one could grasp without hearing the words; and solo piano pieces . . . and sonatas for violin and piano; string quartets—and every work so distinct from the other that each seemed to flow from a different source. . . . May the highest Power strengthen him for what expectation warrants, for there also abides in him another genius—that of modesty. His colleagues greet him upon his first entrance into the world, where perhaps wounds await him, but also palms and laurels. . . .*

Schumann's praise and his prophecy for Brahms's future were so enthusiastic that musicians who read the article could hardly wait to hear the young pianist's compositions. The article aroused in the public and in music critics the expectation of hearing something absolutely extraordinary. But unfortunately it also aroused envy and jealousy in some musicians.

Brahms followed Schumann's suggestion about seeking publication. When he got to Leipzig, he found that Breitkopf & Härtel had some misgivings about publishing the music of an unknown young composer, despite what Robert Schumann had written to them. However, no sooner did the publishers hear him play his compositions than their doubts disappeared. They were charmed by the simple, unaffected "Young Eagle"; and as Brahms became better known in Leipzig, his unassuming and attractive manner and his indifference to the jealousy among the various musical factions disarmed them. He was invited to play at the homes of leading citizens and also played publicly during the week he was in Leipzig, making a number of good friends there through his talent and attractive personality.

Hedwig Salamon, a friend of the Schumanns in Leipzig, wrote:

> *Yesterday a young man came in who held in his hand a letter from Joachim. He sat down opposite me, this young hero of the day, this young Messiah of Schumann's, fair, delicate-looking, who at twenty has clear-cut features free from all passion. Purity, innocence, naturalness, power and depth— this is his nature. One is inclined to think him ridiculous and to judge him harshly because of Schumann's prophecy; but all is forgotten; one can only love and admire him. He spoke with real enthusiasm of books and said, "I spend all my money on books; books are my greatest pleasure. I have read as much as I possibly could since I was small, and have made my way*

without guidance from the worst to the best. . . ."

As he has been able to bear his elevation from obscurity to the perilous position of an idol without losing his modesty, or even his naivete, so God who created such a beautiful nature must continue to sustain him!

In December 1853 an "open letter" was published in Leipzig describing Brahms's first public appearance there. Various composers, teachers, musicians, artists, and poets gathered at an "at home" concert sponsored by Breitkopf & Härtel. The open letter said:

We had occasion to hear young Brahms from Hamburg, referred to the other day in Schumann's article in your journal. This article had caused dubious feelings in numerous circles (perhaps in many cases only from fear). At all events it had fomented a very difficult situation for the young man, for its justification required the fulfillment of great expectations; and when the thin, blond youth appeared, so lacking in presence, so shy, so modest . . . who could have suspected that genius lay behind this unassuming facade? But Schumann was justified; and when Berlioz, deeply moved, embraced the youth and pressed him to his heart, then . . . I felt myself affected by such an exalted mood of enthusiasm as I have seldom experienced.

Brahms wrote to Schumann:

Honored Master:
You have made me so tremendously happy that I can-

not begin to thank you in words. God grant that my works may soon prove to you how much your affection and kindness have encouraged and stimulated me. The public praise you have given me will have directed general expectation so upon my performances that I do not know how I shall be able to do justice to it. Above all it obliges me to take the greatest care in the selection of what is to be published. . . . I should also like to thank you a thousand times for the portrait that you have sent to me as well as for the letter you wrote to my father. By writing it you have made a pair of good people happy for life.

Your

Brahms

A music critic present said of the December concert, "There is something overpowering, something transporting in the works which Brahms performed the other night, a maturity rare in one so young, a creative power springing spontaneously from a deep font of genius. We find ourselves in the presence of one of those highly gifted individuals, an artist by the grace of God. Brahms's spirit is in affinity with the genius of Schumann."

After being in Leipzig, Brahms wrote Schumann:

I have only the best and most satisfactory news to relate. To your warm recommendation I owe my reception in Leipzig, friendly beyond all expectation and especially beyond all deserving. Breitkopf & Härtel declared themselves ready, with great pleasure, to print my first attempts. They are these: "Sonata in C Major," Opus 1; "Sonata in F♯ Minor," Opus 2;

"Songs," Opus 3; and the "Scherzo in E♭ Minor," Opus 4.

I delivered to Mr. Seuff [of Breitkopf & Härtel] the "Sonata in A Minor" for violin and piano, Opus 5; and "Six Songs," Opus 6. May I venture to place Frau Schumann's name on the title page of my second work? I scarcely dare to do so, and yet I should like so much to offer you a small token of my respect and gratitude. It is likely that I shall receive copies of my first things before Christmas. With what feelings shall I then see my parents again after nearly a year's separation! I cannot tell what is in my heart when I think of it.

May you never regret what you have done for me; may I become really worthy of you!

Your
Brahms

As soon as Breitkopf & Härtel paid him for the compositions they accepted, Brahms wrote home about it, sending his family most of the money. As always, even when he became famous and important, his first thought was of his parents, wishing to share with them the good news and whatever he earned.

At Christmas Jakob and Christiane were tremendously proud and happy to see their son's music in print. They noticed that Brahms had dedicated one sonata to Joachim and one to Clara.

"But how is it that you have dedicated nothing to Robert Schumann, to whom you owe so much?" asked his mother, in consternation.

"Because, dear Mama, I don't consider my compositions

good enough yet to dedicate anything to him. I shall certainly do so when I think one of my works is worthy of honoring him."

Christiane was deeply moved when she heard the newly published romantic songs, and she realized that her son had set some of his favorite poems to music. This year's Christmas was an especially joyous one with the great excitement of seeing Brahms's compositions in print. It was pleasant, too, because his parents had rented a slightly better apartment and because Jakob had obtained a better position at the town theatre. Relatives and friends came to see the composer and his family, congratulating him on his success.

Brahms could hardly wait to see his teachers, Marxsen and Cossel, and to tell them about everything. Marxsen, hearing of the triumph in Leipzig, had written a friend, "There was perhaps only one man who was not surprised—myself. I knew what Brahms had accomplished . . . what exalted talent had been bestowed on him, and how finely its flower was unfolding."

Brahms also went to visit the proprietors of the taverns and dance halls he had formerly played in. It was still hard for him to believe that his concert tour with Reményi had suddenly transformed his reputation. He had left Hamburg unknown and had returned nine months later accepted by some of the great musicians of the day.

Schumann's recognition and admiration of Brahms was a great joy to Marxsen. It gave him the satisfaction of knowing that he, as a teacher, had chosen the right way to protect the individuality of Brahms's talent, and to bring it to fruition.

51

As a Christmas present, Brahms sent the first copies of his published compositions to Robert and Clara Schumann, with a letter saying:

I herewith presume to send you your foster children (which owe their right of world citizenship to you). . . . In their new clothes they appear to me far too orderly, almost pedantic. I still cannot get used to seeing these innocent children of nature in such respectable garb.

I look forward with joy to seeing you in Hanover, so that I can tell you in person how much my parents and I are obliged to you and to Joachim for the most blessed time of our lives. I found my parents and teachers most happy and I am spending the most joyous times in their midst.

Then to Joachim he wrote:

I am thinking of coming to Hanover on January 3rd, and so I am not bothering to send you the sonata and first book of songs. I will also save for then news of my wonderful new experiences. My parents, my teachers and I are in seventh heaven. . . . We long for you to share our joy!

This was a Christmas like none other Brahms had ever known.

{ 5 }

The Tragedy

In January 1854, Brahms went to Hanover to visit Joachim. He obtained a room and began working on his "B♭ Major Trio" for piano, violin, and cello. During this period Joachim received a letter from Schumann saying:

Where is Johannes? Is he with you? If so, greet him. Is he flying high—or only down among the flowers? Is he setting drums and trumpet to work yet? He must call to mind the beginning of the Beethoven symphonies; he must try to

*do something of the same sort. The beginning is the main
point; when one has begun well, the end seems to come by
itself. . . .*

At Joachim's home Brahms met Hans von Bülow, a splendid pianist and conductor who had married Liszt's daughter Cosima. Bülow thought so highly of Brahms's compositions that he soon performed one of his works in Hamburg. He spoke of Brahms's lovable, frank nature and praised his talent.

Late in the month of January, Robert and Clara Schumann came to Hanover for a week. There was to be a Schumann Festival with Joachim conducting Schumann's *Fourth Symphony* and Joachim playing Schumann's recently written "Violin Fantasia." What glorious days they were for Brahms, and how the Schumanns loved and encouraged him! After they left for Düsseldorf, Brahms returned to Hamburg to work quietly at home.

Suddenly, in the middle of February, Brahms received the terrible news that Robert had had a nervous breakdown. Obsessed by strange sounds from which he could not free himself, he had tried to end his life in the Rhine. Apparently his illness had been coming on for some time without his friends being aware of it.

Clara, expecting her eighth child in June, was frantic at her beloved husband's illness and at his being taken to a mental asylum in Endenich, near Bonn. Brahms immediately rushed to be with her in Düsseldorf, and from time to time after his concerts, Joachim came to see if he could be of help, too. The shock to Schumann's friends and to people in the musical world was enormous. The doctors would not allow Clara to visit him lest the sight of her aggravate Robert's illness and excite him to violence. She was beside herself and wrote a friend, "Brahms is my dearest, truest support. Since the beginning of Robert's illness he has never left me, but has gone through everything with me and shared my sufferings."

Brahms was like a devoted son to Clara. He had always thought of his own mother as the nourishing, helping, and guiding force in his life, and he transferred some of this feeling to Clara Schumann. Now that she was awaiting the baby that would be born in a few months, he saw how deeply she suffered without her adored Robert. She had been married to him for twelve years against the strong objections of her father, Friedrich Wieck, a well-known piano teacher in Leipzig. Clara had studied music from the time she was a little girl. She had given her first concert when she was nine, with such success that she was proclaimed a prodigy. She had continued to give concerts up to the time of her marriage and was the great pride of her father whose wife, her mother, had left him with their two sons and daughter.

At the age of twenty, Robert Schumann had given up his law studies at the university to study with Clara's father, since he was more interested in music than in anything else. He lived in Wieck's house for two years. At first he paid no special attention to Clara, who was still only a little girl; but as time went on he found her growing into an attractive young woman, and he admired her talent and charm.

With growing concern and possessiveness, Clara's father noticed Robert's interest in his precious daughter. When

55

Robert, after an accident to his hand, left their home to make his way as a composer and began writing love letters to Clara, her father forbade the correspondence and tried to intercept the letters. There were angry scenes, because Clara returned Robert's love and her father had forbidden them to see each other. Later, when Robert asked Herr Wieck to give his consent to their marriage, he absolutely refused. As there was no hope of his agreeing, Robert finally took the matter to court, for Clara was a minor and he had to prove that he was a fit and responsible person in order to marry her. He eventually succeeded in getting a court order allowing him to marry Clara, and since then she had not seen her father. There was bitterness on both sides, but from time to time Clara visited her sympathetic mother, who had remarried and lived in Berlin.

With all they had endured at the hands of Clara's father, and the length of time they had been kept apart, the Schumanns' devotion and attachment were all the greater once they were married. So when the doctors at the mental hospital would not allow Clara to come and see her husband, it was like reliving the tortured days with her father prior to her marriage.

Robert's condition varied, and sometimes Brahms was permitted to visit him; then he could bring Clara news of her beloved husband. When Robert appeared calm and normal he would ask for Clara and the children and recall many happy events of the past. He requested certain books and music, and sent his love to Clara. How happy it made her, but how bitterly she wept!

To distract Clara from her grief, Brahms would play his

new compositions for her: a trio he was completing and a sonata for two pianos which later became the "Piano Concerto in D Minor." On Robert's forty-fourth birthday Clara was particularly desolate that her husband still had to remain in the mental hospital. She was told that a visit from her might cause a dangerous relapse; despite this she did not lose hope that he would recover and come home.

Brahms's devotion and loyalty helped Clara to become calmer after the first terrible days; but the only money she had to live on was the small salary from the Düsseldorf orchestra of which Robert had been conductor for a short time. Not only were there all the children to be supported, but the fees of doctors and expenses of the mental hospital had to be met. Clara was too proud to accept gifts or charity from friends and outsiders who offered to help her.

During all this time Brahms's only income was from his published compositions and a few piano pupils; but in the summer when people went away for vacations there was naturally less income from his students. He would so much have liked to be able to support Clara and her children. To celebrate Robert's birthday, and thinking it would cheer Clara, he composed a set of piano pieces based on Hungarian tunes he had learned earlier from Reményi on their concert tour, and left them at the door of her room.

Clara's new baby, born in June of 1854, was named Felix after Felix Mendelssohn, who had been conductor of the symphony orchestra in Leipzig. He had befriended the Schumanns and had done a great deal to make Robert's compositions known to the public. Apart from his remarkable musicianship, they had loved Mendelssohn as a warm and highly gifted person.

In honor of the birth of her little son and to divert Clara during her convalescence, Brahms played for her the "Variations for Piano on a Theme by Robert Schumann," dedicated to her. She wrote in her diary: "Johannes tried to bring comfort to my heart. He composed variations on the beautiful intimate theme which made such a deep impression upon me a year ago, and touched me deeply with his tender thoughtfulness."

Since the Schumann children often asked him to make up songs for them, he gathered together some he had composed, and some folk tunes to which he had added accompaniments. He called them "Children's Folk Songs," dedicating them "To the Children of Robert and Clara Schumann." In this collection is "The Little Sandman," based on the tune he sang as a child, *"In Bethlehem Transeamus."*

The flowers have long been sleeping beneath the pale moonshine. Their tiny heads are nodding upon their stalks so fine. The rose tree bends her dreamy head, and shakes her petals red. Slumber, slumber, my own sweet baby dear!

It was a consolation to Clara that her friendship with Brahms stimulated him to compose so much. It was good to feel she could help the kind young man of twenty-one, who had been reared in less privileged circumstances than hers. She took as much pride in him as in any child of her family; and what a comfort it was to have him nearby, sustaining her through the dark days! With Robert away what would she have done without him? In her diary she wrote:

> *. . . I prefer to speak of Robert to Brahms more than anyone else, primarily because Robert loved him so, and also on account of that sensitivity which, despite his youth, does me so much good! His entire personality is impressive, with a maturity far beyond his years; yet on the other hand his emotions are those of a naive child. . . .*

In August she went to Ostend on the Belgian coast to recuperate from the birth of the baby and to alleviate her sorrow over Robert. With his strong attachment to Clara, Brahms missed her sorely. His reverence and respect for her as a beautiful woman, mother and musician were boundless. Sometimes he called her "dear Mama," his love for her seeming as genuine as that for his own mother. He was willing to give up everything to be at her side; and when she decided to go on a concert tour again to earn money to support her seven living children and to pay Robert's expenses, Brahms assured her he would gladly stay in her home to look after the children and supervise the household so that she would have no need to worry.

Although his piano lessons brought in too little money, he absolutely refused to give public concerts when invited to do so because it would take him away from Clara's family. His parents, consulting with Brahms's old piano teacher Marxsen, were greatly disturbed that he had buried himself in Düsseldorf as a babysitter and was doing nothing to further himself as a pianist and composer. They thought it was too great a sacrifice he was making for the Schumanns.

However, Brahms wished for nothing more than to devote his life to Clara. Only when she was to play in Hamburg in November was he willing to leave her house, and then he wrote to his mother that they were coming; Christiane was delighted at the prospect of their visit and answered:

> *Oh, how wonderful, how splendid that you are going to visit us and that the good Frau Schumann is also coming to Hamburg! How delighted we shall be to see her! You will decide, as you know her best, if we should offer to put her up. It does look better here than it did last year, when the old kitchen range stood in the living room and Elise was ill. . . . Come to us very soon and stay for a long time. But please write when you are coming so that we can make the thick oatmeal cakes that you like so much. . . .*

Although Clara did not accept the invitation to stay with Brahms's parents, she often took her meals with his family and felt much at home with the "simple and respectable people," as she described them. She was especially drawn to Brahms's mother, because her son had grown so dear to her.

Now that Clara had decided to become a concert pianist again, she practiced with as great purpose and energy as she had done before she married. It was not easy to regain the facility she had lost during the twelve years she was wife and mother. Naturally she worried, even with Hannes there, about the welfare of the children while she was away. So her mother, living in Berlin, took nine-year-old Julie to live with her. The older girls, Marie and Elise, could help the new governess, Bertha, with the school-age boys; and Eugenie and baby Felix would have a nurse to themselves.

However, even these arrangements would not bring peace to her mind unless Brahms were there to watch over them all. She knew how much the children meant to him and they in turn adored him. Reassured by him, she practiced night and day to get her fingers and wrists in good condition again for her concert tours. She wrote in her diary:

I am haunted by music as never before; at night I cannot sleep, and by day I am so absorbed by music that I lose track of all else. . . .

For her thirty-fifth birthday on September 13th, 1854, Brahms prepared a little concert for her to be given by her two older daughters, Marie and Elise, as a surprise. He had coached them in secret, and although they had no real talent, their earnestness and desire to work hard to please their mother meant a great deal to Clara.

On this birthday Robert Schumann's condition seemed so much better that he was allowed to receive a letter from Clara, which he answered the next day. He wrote:

Endenich, September 14, 1854

How I rejoice, beloved Clara, to see your handwriting. Many thanks for writing to me that you and the dear children still remember me. Greet and kiss the little ones! Oh, if I could only see and speak to you again! There is so much I would like to know: how your life is going on: where you are living and if you still play as gloriously as formerly. . . . What joyful news you have again sent me . . . that Brahms, to whom you must give my kind and admiring greetings, has come to live in Düsseldorf. What friendship! If you would like to know whose is my favorite name, you will no doubt guess his, the unforgettable one! What have Brahms and Joachim been composing? . . .

Robert had seemed so improved that as Christmas Eve approached Clara kept hoping that her dear husband would return to surprise them. She listened constantly for the brass knocker on the door to announce his arrival. When she had nearly lost hope, a knock sounded. Flushed and excited, she flew to the door—to find that it was only Brahms, smiling happily at her with his arms overflowing with packages.

Clara did her best to hide her disappointment, and Brahms, heartsick for her, pretended not to notice. What would he not have given then to have been Robert instead of himself! The children clung to Brahms, who amused them with tricks on the piano and told exciting stories. Clara, sadder then ever, could hardly bear to join the Christmas Eve celebration.

⚜ [6] ⚜

A Friend of the Family

The only things that saved Clara from utter despair were the practicing and memorizing sessions for her concert tours. The music would be her salvation and that of the family, too. Sometimes she grew more confident of Robert's recovery, only to be disappointed again and again.

Usually Brahms spent Christmas with his parents no matter where he happened to be; but this year he preferred to spend it with Clara. It was the first time he had stayed away from home. Clara wrote his mother:

My dear Frau Brahms:

I have robbed you of your dear Johannes, just now at Christmas time. I cannot deny myself the pleasure of sending him to you in a portrait, which I hope will give you pleasure, and which may sometimes remind you of myself and my dearest husband, who will cherish Johannes all his life with true affection. This assurance may be some little consolation to your mother's heart when he is far away from you.

Yours very sincerely,
Clara Schumann

Her gratitude to Brahms was unbounded. He helped the little ones with their schoolwork and was nursemaid to the smaller children when the servants had a day off. He even did the family shopping, willing to do anything that would ease Clara's burden and free her for the music which was now her greatest happiness.

No sooner was it known that Clara was available for concerts than she was besieged by invitations from everywhere to come and play. Some of the places remembered her playing there when she was younger. Some, knowing about her tragedy, asked her to come out of sympathy for her as the wife of Robert Schumann. England, where she had never played, was particularly eager to hear her. There were requests from German cities, from Austria-Hungary, Holland, Belgium, and France too. It was very gratifying to know that she was still valued as a concert pianist. Now that her household could be left safely in Brahms's hands she started her tour in Vienna.

She overwhelmed the audiences and critics by her superb

playing. She performed a great many of Robert's compositions and some of Brahms's; then she went on to other cities with equal success. While she was in Dresden to give a concert she had a reunion with her estranged father who had since remarried. He suggested that since she would be away from home so much giving concerts, he would be glad to have Marie and Elise come to stay with him. It would be nice to know his granddaughters. Clara was pleased with the idea; with Julie in Berlin with her grandmother and these two girls in Dresden, it would leave only Ludwig, eight, Ferdinand, seven, Eugenie, five, and the baby Felix for Brahms and the servants to look after.

She particularly enjoyed her concert tour in England because she was such a great success among the warmhearted English people. But everywhere she went she anxiously awaited letters from Brahms giving her news of Robert. Mostly the news she received was disquieting, but sometimes she was cheered to hear of Brahms finding Robert somewhat improved.

At Clara's insistence, Brahms began playing again in public. She, Brahms, and Joachim gave a concert together in Danzig in the autumn of 1855, followed by performances at Bremen, Leipzig, and Hamburg. Brahms's reputation as a pianist was increasing and he was composing a great deal. There were ballades for piano, the first movement of the *Symphony in C Minor,* and the "Piano Quartet in C Minor." Often Brahms felt the need for better grounding in counterpoint, where many voices harmonize agreeably, each one a complete musical expression in its own right. The wonderful contrapuntal way in which Bach wrote was his great model.

Wishing to improve his contrapuntal writing, he made a pact with Joachim that once a week they should exchange problems in counterpoint. They would work out the exercises and send them to each other to be corrected. If one of them failed to keep the agreement he would have to pay a fine. Joachim never seemed to have the time to work on his own contrapuntal problems and preferred paying the fines, which Hannes used to buy books for himself. However, Brahms was more persistent and kept at the problems he set himself.

But it soon turned out that Brahms was receiving too much money in fines for books from Joachim, and so Brahms wrote him he would much prefer seeing his work than receiving the fines. This produced results, and Joachim wrote:

> To keep my word, here are the desired contrapuntal solutions on a given theme. . . . It was a difficult task, and compared with your meaningful ones, my canons are rather muddy and unsure in their rhythmic as well as their melodic execution. I repeat: have patience with my lack of skill in such things.

Then to a friend Joachim wrote:

> Some time ago I started a kind of musical correspondence with Brahms; we send each other assignments of considerable difficulty. This type of musical interchange with him means a great deal to me: I remain in intellectually close contact with someone in whom I take the most keen interest. My friend, although younger than I am, is already most accom-

plished in the manipulation of this type of composition, whereas I never occupied myself with it beyond the basic necessities. In this way I also acquire some artistic stimulation.

The one who benefited most from these exercises was Brahms, and it advanced his skill in writing contrapuntal music. Joachim, although a performer rather than a composer, could be an excellent adviser. He was never jealous of Brahms and tried always to promote his compositions by playing them. Brahms would not permit any of his orchestral compositions to be published until Joachim gave him his valuable criticism, so great a confidence did he have in Joachim's judgments and advice.

On Brahms's twenty-third birthday, May 7, 1856, his mother wrote him:

> *I don't know what you are doing at this moment. I'm all alone and would like to talk to you a little. . . . Tonight we were all rather jolly; we drank to the health of all of you, especially that of the poor sick man. Johannes dear, if we only had the power to do something for the good Schumann! I beg you not to take his illness too much to heart; you cannot help him, and it only does you harm. . . .*
>
> *Your tenderly loving*
> *Mother*

While Clara was in Holland, Brahms wrote her that the doctors were not very optimistic about her husband's condition.

Brahms had not been allowed to see Robert Schumann for several months, and when he did, the shock of seeing his friend so changed and failing so fast shook him. Nevertheless Clara had to go on to London to give her concerts. Her family's livelihood depended on them. She wrote in her diary:

I played yesterday at the Philharmonic with a bleeding heart. I read hopelessness between the lines [of Brahms's letter] as regards my beloved husband. . . . Whence came the power to play I do not know. . . .

In July 1856, when Clara returned from England, Brahms was waiting for her in Antwerp to make her homecoming less desolate. There was increasingly bad news about Robert. Reaching Düsseldorf, Clara found her children in good health and in high spirits, eager to show her all the new tricks they had learned from Brahms. She begged the doctors to let her see Robert but they again refused, saying that the unexpected sight of her might lead to serious consequences and that they could not guarantee his recovery.

Greatly fatigued from worry and her concert tours, she decided to have a little vacation and went to a resort at the seashore not far from Hamburg. On her way there she stayed overnight with the Brahms family for the first time, and they felt highly honored. Afterwards she wrote Christiane:

From here, my dear friend, I can send you little or no good news. I am feeling the separation from Johannes too painfully and I am leading the most solitary life. Dusterbrock [the resort] is lovely, it is true, but simply because it is so lovely, it is all the more painful that I must enjoy it alone, without my beloved husband and without the dearest friend I have in the world—and this Johannes is. If he were with me, I could bear it, more easily. . . . You made me so comfortable that day in Hamburg that I now feel doubly lonely.

Shortly after this there came a telegram from her husband's doctors saying that she could visit him. She had not seen Robert for two and a half years. To her sorrow and dismay, when she got there the doctors decided it would be better that she not see him after all, because of his highly excited state. She returned to Düsseldorf; a few days later she was summoned to Endenich immediately. Robert was dying. With Brahms she entered his room and saw her beloved husband lying quietly with his eyes closed. He sensed her presence, awoke and recognized Clara kneeling beside his bed.

She later wrote in her diary:

I saw him. It was in the evening between six and seven o'clock. He smiled and with the greatest effort, for he scarcely had control of his limbs, put his arm around me. I shall never forget this. . . . Everything around him seemed sacred to me, even the very air he breathed. On Monday, the 28th [of July], Johannes and I spent the whole day there, partly with him, but often just watching through a peephole in the wall.

The following day Robert's death came quietly, and that night Clara entered in her diary:

70

I have no love left. He has taken it all with him. All happiness has departed from me with his passing. Another life has now begun for me.

Brahms sent a telegram to Joachim to come; the funeral was to be held in Bonn. Long lines of musicians and music-lovers, accompanied by a band of brass instruments, followed Schumann's body to the cemetery where beautiful old German chorales were played.

Clara, a widow at the age of thirty-seven, was full of anguish. She returned to Düsseldorf to her children, Brahms and Joachim by her side to comfort and help her as best they could. Brahms set to work putting Schumann's papers and music in order, writing and answering letters for Clara. Joachim wrote to Liszt:

Frau Schumann returned here yesterday; the presence of her children and of Brahms, whom Schumann loved like a son, comforts the noble lady, who appears to me in her deep grief a lofty example of God-given strength.

Not long after Robert's death, Brahms decided to go back to Hamburg. It was no longer proper for an unmarried young man to be living in Clara's household. Sorrowfully she walked with him to the railroad station. When she came home she wrote in her diary:

It was like returning from another funeral.

From Hamburg Brahms sent Clara frequent letters showing how much he missed her and the children:

> *Send me news of you, as it is my greatest joy. . . .*
> *To you I now repeat that you and your husband are the*
> *most beautiful experience of my life. You signify its greatest*
> *enrichment and most noble content.*

❦{7}❧

𝒜 Court Musician

After Robert's funeral, exhausted by her grief, Clara felt she must go somewhere to rest and have a change. She decided to go to Switzerland with two of her sons, and invited Brahms and his sister Elise to go with them. Brahms came to Düsseldorf by himself first and then returned to bring Elise with him later on. Clara, filled with a warm personal attachment to the whole Brahms family as well as to him, wrote his mother suggesting what Elise would need for the trip.

It was the first journey away from home for Elise and it

opened a new world to her. They traveled up the Rhine, stayed for several weeks in the village of Gersau overlooking Lake Lucerne; they went on to Lake Constance, and then back to Heidelberg in Germany. Being with Clara made Elise love and admire her more than ever. Now that Clara was free to marry again Elise often wondered why her brother, who seemed full of such joy and peace when beside her, did not ask Clara to become his wife. It was true that Clara was fourteen years older than Brahms; but hadn't their own mother been seventeen years older than their father? It did not seem so unusual to Elise.

However, either because Brahms did not wish to or because he could not bring himself to, he preferred to be Clara's adoring, protecting, and devoted friend for the rest of his days. To be able to count on that would be happiness enough for him.

Shortly after her thirty-eighth birthday, Clara moved to Berlin where she had been offered a teaching position at the Conservatory of Music. It would be a solace to be near her mother and live in a big city away from her sad memories. Nevertheless, without Robert and Brahms she felt just as miserable there as she had in Düsseldorf. Realizing her unhappiness, Brahms wrote:

You must try seriously to take care that your sad mood does not grow excessive and interminable. Life is precious. Mental depression works powerful destruction in the body. Don't persuade yourself that life means little to you. This is not true. . . . If you should surrender completely to such

74

moods you will also fail to enjoy whatever good things come your way. . . . To what end has the heavenly gift of hope been bestowed on mankind? . . . You must decide every morning quite earnestly and simply to be more equable and cheerful, that day as well as at all other times. . . .

Brahms now took over some of the piano lessons Clara used to give to pupils from the Detmold Court. Detmold was on the east slope of the remarkable Teutoburger Forest, about one hundred and fifty miles south of Hamburg. It was in Detmold in 783 that the troops of Charlemagne and the Saxons had fought. In 1857, Brahms had been invited to Detmold to give a concert at the court. This was such a great success that he was asked to come in the autumn to play, to give lessons to the Princess Friedericke, and to conduct an amateur choral society which would meet each week at the castle. The Prince, his brothers and sisters would be members, too. The position was to last for three months, September, October, and November, with no duties in the morning so he would have time to compose. Brahms was attracted by the possibility of having the Prince's orchestra at his disposal to try out his instrumental works, and the choral group available for his songs and choral compositions. It would be a great opportunity, as it was for Haydn with his orchestra and singers when he was in the employ of the Princes Estherházy. In modern times composers seldom have such an advantage. He decided to accept the position.

It had been difficult to tear himself away from Clara and her children, but it was now time to make up his mind to work

75

hard and be independent. After all, he was already twenty-four years old; either he would have to give concerts and offer piano lessons to make a living, or he would have to take the Detmold offer. This would at least cover his modest needs for a time and make it possible for him to compose.

He told Clara, "Now I feel I can take in my stride many things that I previously had to toil over. How fine it is to create with unimpaired vigor!"

He soon found that his decision had been a good one. The mornings at Detmold were entirely free, and he used his time to compose, practice, and walk in the ancient forest where the picturesque, turreted castle was situated. The towering trees, the luxuriant greenery, the autumn flowers, the birds and small animals he encountered gave him much happiness and inspiration. He felt himself grow more cheerful despite his painful separation from Clara.

Here, as he walked in the solitude of the Teutoburger Forest, he felt full of a creative urge again. He was always stimulated by the beauty of the countryside, just as Beethoven had been. Brahms composed best in the midst of nature, and his surroundings now inspired him to write two charming orchestral serenades and to work again on his "Piano Concerto in D Minor," which he had thought of making into a symphony earlier. He read a great deal, too, and said, "Whoever wishes to play well must not only practice a great deal, but must also read many books."

This first season at Detmold was gratifying, both to the court and to himself, so that when they invited him to return the next year he accepted gladly and promised to return in the autumn.

76

Shortly after leaving Detmold, he received a letter from the Cologne Conservatory offering him a position there. They told him the burden of teaching would not be too heavy and that his colleagues would be friendly. Besides, they pointed out, he would be in a big city and not buried in the country, as he now was. Brahms had to admit that to a certain extent he *was* buried in Detmold, beautiful as it was. There were only two people there who interested him, the first violinist of the court orchestra and the musical son of the Court Marshal; and as he did not enjoy fuss and ceremony he kept aloof from the members of the nobility. He had written home in a merry mood:

> *The other day I conducted my choral society, which is richly adorned with Serene Highnesses, without a necktie! Luckily I didn't feel embarrassed or annoyed, since I only noticed it when I was going to bed!*

Brahms decided against the position in Cologne because it would take away too much time from composing, and he returned to Hamburg to stay until the summer. His family had moved to better quarters due to the generous amounts of money he sent home. He now thought of his friend Otto Grimm in Göttingen, whom he had met five years before when he visited Joachim. Grimm had just been appointed musical director in Göttingen. Brahms went to visit him there in the summer of 1858. It was much more enjoyable to be with less aristocratic friends, making music together and discussing books.

While at Göttingen, during a musical evening at Grimm's house, he became acquainted with Agathe von Siebold, the daughter of a professor of medicine at the university. Brahms found her a little plain but very charming and lively, with an excellent singing voice "like that of a rare Amati violin," as he described it. She had sung him one of Brahms's own songs, which flattered and delighted him. In no time at all Brahms lost his heart to her. Years later she wrote in her "Recollections" that those were "the lovely summer days transfigured by the glory of love."

Brahms and "Gathe," as he called her, were together a great deal and appeared extremely happy in each other's company. He loved her sense of humor, her dark sparkling eyes, her lovely voice; indeed, everything about her. Like him she enjoyed wandering over the rolling hills, reading books, and making music. All this was a strong bond between them; but it was mainly the way she sang Brahms's lovely songs, "By the Window," "The Blacksmith," and "Sonnet," that attracted him. Poetry had a great hold on Brahms's imagination. Next to the Bible it was Goethe, the great poet, who inspired him most in his songs.

During the summer Clara decided to come and visit Brahms in Göttingen with five of her children because, she said, now that they were apart and she lived in Berlin it would be delightful to spend a few weeks of every summer near each other. Suddenly she became aware of Brahms's great interest and attachment to Gathe and noticed how he put his arm tenderly around her waist. She could not help feeling a pang of envy and left Göttingen quite abruptly. Brahms, surprised at her sudden departure, stayed on so he could be with Gathe until the very last moment, when his duties at Detmold would tear him away from her.

Because he missed Gathe once he was back in Detmold, his letters home began to show that he was not finding life there as congenial as before, and his mother, sensitive to his moods, realized it. She wrote:

> *You find it so narrow and boring there . . . and say that you would like to run away. Last year you found it easier. You have been spoiled at Göttingen.*

Brahms certainly longed for his Gathe, and to appease his yearning he wrote more songs for her, such as "Parting," "Yearning," "The Kiss," and "Serenade."

Lento   SERENADE (from a folk song)

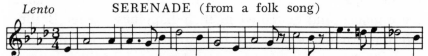

Good night, good night, my dearest dear, good night and sweetly sleep. And o'er thy rest may angel hosts a faithful vigil keep. Good night, good night, I softly sigh, the night-wind lull thee off to sleep. Sleep sound and dream of me this night, who watch for thee, who wait for thee, my longing heart's delight. Who cannot sleep for loving thee, who art my heart's, my soul's delight.

He did not try to hide his deep attachment to Gathe from the Grimms when he wrote to them in Göttingen, and Frau Grimm replied:

> *Your dear letter has just arrived. . . . Many thanks for it. I will send it at once to Agathe. She will be greatly pleased. But now I have a strange request to make. I should like to*

give Agathe a portrait of you for Christmas, but I have none.
It would be very charming of you, my dear Johannes, if you
would send me one. I should like to have it framed. But if you
would like to give it to her yourself, I have nothing against
that; I only want Agathe to get one, as I know how delighted
she would be.

Brahms did not have a picture to send her, and as there
was no artist in Detmold whom he could commission to draw
or paint his portrait, he was unable to fulfil this request.

At the end of his second season in Detmold, which had
seemed unendurably long this time, Brahms rushed back to
Göttingen to spend ten days with Gathe. How happy he was to
see her again! Everyone in the university town knew about
the romance and delighted in their happiness. After Brahms
left, the Grimms expected to hear from him that he and Gathe
were officially engaged, but when he remained silent Grimm
wrote asking about it. He pointed out that Brahms should
either make his attachment to Gathe official or not see her
again, since he was placing her in an awkward position.
Brahms found himself in a dilemma and finally wrote to her,
"I love you! I must see you again! But I cannot wear fet-
ters. . . ."

Naturally Agathe was deeply wounded, and she wrote
Brahms telling him she would not see him again. She had her
pride, too. For many years they thought of each other with
deep affection; and later when he composed his "Second String
Sextet" he dedicated it to her in a subtle way by having the
first and second violins in the first movement play the notes

80

that spelled out her name—excepting that the letter H in her name became a B natural, as it is in German musical notation. Brahms confessed to a friend in connection with the sextet, "Here I have freed myself from my last love." The fact was that Brahms loved music more than he could love a woman enough to marry her.

Ten years after parting from Brahms, Agathe got married; and it was only when she was an old woman that she showed her forgiveness by sending a greeting to him through Joachim. In her "Recollections" she later wrote,

But the memory of her great love for the young man, of the days of her youth, glowing with poetry and beauty, has never faded. . . . Over and over again his immortal work has contributed to her happiness. He, however, strode by on his path to fame, and as he, like every genius, belonged to humanity, she gradually learned to appreciate his wisdom in severing the bonds which had threatened to fetter him. She saw clearly at last that she could never have filled his life with her love.

The loss of Agathe was somewhat eased by having his "Piano Concerto in D Minor," a rather grim, unhappy, and unfriendly work, performed in public. He played it in Hanover, with Joachim conducting, and shortly thereafter in Leipzig, where it was not received with much enthusiasm. He wrote to Clara about it, saying:

My concerto went very well. I had two rehearsals. You

have probably already heard that it was a complete fiasco; at the rehearsal it met with total silence, and at the performance (where hardly three people raised their hands to clap) it was actually hissed. But all this made no impression on me. I quite enjoyed the rest of the music and did not think of my concerto.

Brahms genuinely believed that its lack of success was a good thing for him because it would force him to buckle down. He said he was still experimenting and groping his way.

Two months later Brahms performed his concerto in Hamburg, Joachim again conducting, but this time the audience was not so cold. On the same program his "First Serenade" was played, and this more warmly received. There followed a musical evening with Joachim, where he met again the extraordinary singer Julius Stockhausen, thirty years old, with whom he had become acquainted three years before in 1855. Because of this man's fine voice, Brahms wrote and dedicated some of his loveliest songs for him, and Stockhausen often sang them in public concerts.

At twenty-five, Brahms was fortunate in having the help of three famous musicians to perform his compositions in public. For his piano music there was Clara; for his orchestral and chamber music he had Joachim as conductor and violinist; and for his songs Stockhausen was the sensitive and artistic singer.

In Hamburg Brahms made more friends than in previous years, among them the conductor of the Hamburg Philharmonic Orchestra. He enjoyed having musical friends in his own city with whom he could talk about music and meet to

I have to add to the causes of this decision that I shall be much occupied this autumn with the publication of my works, with revising the proofs of some and preparing others for the engraver. On this account alone, therefore, I must decide to stay here during the winter. I particularly desire to express my regret to Princess Friedericke that I shall be unable to enjoy her progress in playing and her great sympathy for music.

At home he no longer found his cramped quarters suitable or quiet enough for working on his compositions. He therefore rented a small apartment in the house of the elderly musical aunt of one of his choirgirls, in the nearby suburb of Hamm. His landlady, Frau Rösing, put the whole house at his disposal, including a splendid grand piano. The lovely garden there and the surrounding countryside suited him perfectly. He was able to finish many things he was working on: piano pieces, "Variations for Four Hands on a Theme by Schumann," and the remarkable "Variations on a Theme of Handel." He completed two piano quartets and composed the first of the songs called the Magelone Romances, which were based on medieval stories he had found in a book at Winsen when he was a boy of fifteen. These he dedicated to the singer Stockhausen. Later he dedicated a piano quartet to Frau Rösing because she had been so kind.

Brahms had always been interested in writing variations, and to become as skillful as possible with them he had studied variations by Beethoven and especially Bach's *Goldberg Variations*, which he loved. There were thirty of these and they had been composed in 1736 for Count Kayserling, Russian Ambassador to the Court of Dresden. Kayserling had loved music passionately, and famous musicians were in his service, among them J. T. Goldberg, a harpsichordist who had been one of Bach's best pupils. Suffering from sleeplessness due to his heavy responsibilities and travels for Catherine the Great, Empress of Russia, the Count had Goldberg play for him to soothe him during the interminable nights. Kayserling had asked Bach to compose a piece which Goldberg might play for him at night.

Bach gladly set to work on what became known as the *Goldberg Variations,* an aria with thirty variations for a two-manual keyboard. For this, Kayserling sent Bach a snuffbox with one hundred goldpieces as a token of his appreciation.

Brahms now composed variations on songs of Handel, Mozart, and other composers, and also variations on original themes of his own. His variations were full of contrast, with changeable tempi and varying meters. From studying Beethoven, he had learned how to deal with the final variation, which summarized one long series of short pieces.

The variation principle, with its spontaneous flow of invention, had a great influence on the structure of Brahms's compositions, and it can also be heard in his symphonies. Even in the two clarinet sonatas written much later, in 1895, Brahms used the variation principle.

The "Four Serious Songs" composed the following year, when Clara died, also show his marvellous invention and technique in the variation form. However, the inner substance of his works was always full of vitality and originality, and not dependent solely on his technical ability to invent variations.

86

Although his works were often played in Germany, it was a pleasant surprise to learn that his "Second Serenade" had been played in February 1862 by the New York Philharmonic Orchestra. It was the first orchestral work of his to be played outside Germany. The early appreciation of Brahms's music in the United States grew each year, and his works were welcomed and performed as they appeared, especially in Boston by the symphony orchestra there. Brahms's chamber music was often performed by the famous Kneisel Quartet of Boston. Today, too, his symphonies are played as often as those of the other great masters.

Brahms was happy in Hamm, and kept hoping something interesting would be offered to keep him in Hamburg. In the spring Clara and her daughter Marie spent a few weeks in Hamburg and attended Brahms's choir practices with him and his "dear girls." They saw how hard he made his Ladies' Choir work, but he was also full of fun and jokes and often went with the choir members on picnics in the country. When his first season with them was over they came to the last practice dressed in black to show their grief.

In a bouquet of flowers they gave him he found a beautiful silver inkstand. He wrote them in thanks saying he hoped to write more songs for them and that he would certainly hear more beautiful melodies resounding around him as he looked at the lovely present which he kept on his writing table. He had already composed for them the "Liebeslieder" or "Love-song Waltzes," "Part Songs from Twelfth Night," and others.

Now and then Brahms went to music festivals in other cities and met celebrities such as Jenny Lind, the singer. It was at the Rhine Festival in Düsseldorf that he became acquainted with the Viennese publisher, Fritz Simrock, who became his publisher and lifelong friend. Simrock urged him to settle in his city just as other great masters—Haydn, Mozart, Beethoven, and Schubert—had done.

Clara and Joachim had also often recommended Vienna to Brahms, pointing out that if he gained prestige there, he would then undoubtedly be much more appreciated by the people of Hamburg and might have a better chance of obtaining the coveted position of conductor of the orchestra. Many Viennese musicians had urged him to come and live there. Now Simrock was insistent that Brahms come to Vienna to give concerts, and he extolled the advantages of the musical city.

Brahms was greatly tempted by all he heard about the city and the warm-hearted musical Viennese, about the gaiety compared to the reserved atmosphere of Hamburg, about the tasty Viennese food, and the excellent concerts both public and private. He would enjoy sitting in the open-air cafes of Vienna, hearing the military bands playing waltzes and dance music, seeing the children at play on the Prater, listening to the gypsy music at Hungarian restaurants, and walking along the Danube. And now that he had a Viennese publisher who was to bring out two of his vocal compositions, a psalm and some duets, it seemed natural to go there. To Grimm he wrote in November 1862:

> Well, this is it! I have established myself here in Vienna within ten paces of the Prater. I can drink my wine where Beethoven drank his!

❦{8}❧

City of Music

Brahms was taken quickly to the hearts of the wide musical circle of Vienna. He was introduced to the interesting musical groups—choruses, chamber music ensembles, orchestras. It was obvious that the large number of excellent singers and instrumentalists at the conservatory of the Friends of Music Society, which trained budding musicians so well, was keeping up the great musical tradition for which Vienna was famous.

Simrock introduced Brahms to many musical people,

among them Gustav Nöttebohm, who wrote articles about Beethoven and Schubert; and to Karl Taussig, a pupil of Liszt and a brilliant young pianist of twenty-two with whom Brahms played his newly completed "F Minor Sonata" for two pianos at a concert of the Vienna Singakademie. It was Taussig's magnificent playing that inspired Brahms to practice the piano more diligently—for he had been neglecting it—and to compose his most brilliant piano composition, the "Variations on a Theme of Paganini."

He also became friendly with C. F. Pohl, the librarian of the Friends of Music Society, with the composer Karl Goldmark, and with many beautiful women—one of them Luise Dustmann, an opera singer who affectionately called him "Hansi." To Clara, who was always advising him to get married, he wrote about a very pretty girl with whom he would have "made a fool of himself" if someone had not snatched her up by Christmas.

Even at the age of thirty, Brahms appeared younger than he was; he was far from being a man of the world, still shy and too modest to promote his own compositions in order to make them known. Despite this he was quickly accepted in Vienna, and one well-known person after another tried to be of help. The celebrated Hellmesberger Quartet invited him to play one of his piano quartets with them. This was such a success that Brahms was proclaimed Beethoven's heir and embraced enthusiastically by the members of the quartet. He was then asked to arrange a concert of his own, which he did. Within a week he performed another of his piano quartets, played his "Variations on a Theme of Handel," and also played works by Bach and Schumann. He wrote to his parents:

I rejoiced yesterday. My concert went very well. The quartet [the "Piano Quartet in A Major"] was well received, and I had great success as a pianist. Each number won rich applause. I felt the enthusiasm in the audience. . . . I played as unconcernedly as though I were at home among my friends. I could earn a lot giving concerts; but I don't want to do so, because it takes up so much time that I would not have time for anything else. The public here is much more responsive than ours at home. You should see how attentive they are and hear their applause! I am delighted that I gave the concert.

This encouraged him to give a second concert of his own and again the audience was greatly impressed by his beautiful piano playing. Most people did not actually understand all his compositions at first hearing, just as happens in the case of modern composers now; but two Viennese conductors were so interested in him that they performed two of his serenades. Jakob and Christiane were delighted to hear of his success, and when at Christmas time they received the reviews from the newspapers telling of his concerts it seemed the best present possible.

Brahms's mother wrote him:

You have so many friends in Vienna already! So you are probably not homesick any longer; otherwise I think you would be guilty of keeping me awake at night.

Later she thanked him for a photograph of himself that looked so gay that she hoped he had found some girl to love and might soon announce his engagement. Like most mothers, she wanted to see her son married.

In the midst of his contentment at being in Vienna, Brahms got news from a Hamburg friend that Stockhausen, although a singer, had been chosen to be conductor of the Hamburg Philharmonic Orchestra to fill the place left vacant by the retirement of the previous conductor. Brahms was terribly disappointed and wrote to Clara:

> *This is a much sadder business for me than you can understand. I am altogether an old-fashioned person. I am not a cosmopolitan, but rather I love my native town as a mother. . . . How glad I should have been to find a permanent niche there! Happy as I am here, with so much that is beautiful to gladden me, I nevertheless feel and shall always feel that I am a stranger and can have no peace.*
>
> *If I am not to hope for anything here, then where? Where should I care to go, even if I had a chance? One wants to be bound, and to acquire the things that make life worth living. One dreads solitude. Working in active association with others, having social intercourse, and family happiness . . . who is so inhuman that he does not long for these things?*

To comfort him Clara pointed out that he was young, talented, and with a brilliant future before him. Wasn't it high time he got married?

"If I had been selected as conductor," answered Brahms, "I could have married and lived like other men."

He now made up his mind to settle permanently in Vienna rather than live in Hamburg; he was sure he would compose more happily in its sympathetic atmosphere. From time to time Brahms went to visit his parents; but noticing a growing strain between them he felt depressed, for he loved them both and did not wish to take sides.

In May 1863, Brahms went to Hanover to visit his old friend Joachim, who was about to be married. His fiancée was an opera singer, Amalie Weiss, and Brahms wanted to hear her last public performance in Gluck's opera *Orpheus*. At that time it was not considered proper for a married woman to appear on the stage in opera. However, she would be able to give concerts, so she would not have to give up her career entirely. Brahms found her velvety alto voice so exquisite that he wrote for her a number of lovely songs which she often sang later, thus helping to make Brahms known. While he was there he also had the opportunity of trying out his "String Quintet in F Minor" with Joachim. This work later became a sonata for two pianos. From there Brahms went to Hamburg to celebrate his thirtieth birthday with his family.

His mother, now seventy-four, was frail and not at all well. His father, however, was still vigorous and active at fifty-seven. Now the parents seemed truly ill-matched. Brahms did not know how to bring peace into his once serene home, and finding it a hopeless situation he was glad to accept an offer from Vienna asking him to return to conduct the Singakademie, a choral society. Shortly after his departure Jakob received a letter:

Father, if things should be going badly with you, music is always the best consolation; go and look into my old copy of Saul [*by Handel*] *and you will find comfort there.*

And one day taking this advice, for he was in trouble finan-
cially, Jakob found to his surprise that there was money between the pages of the score. The bank-notes were certainly an
effective remedy.

Six weeks later, in November, Brahms had prepared the
choral group so well that they were able to give a concert consisting of a Bach cantata, a Beethoven work for voices, several
of his own arrangements of folk songs, and a choral work by
Schumann. It was a great success and the music critics wrote
appreciative articles about the new conductor. Brahms had
shown exceptional knowledge of the music and style of older
composers such as Bach at this performance, and he planned
to present other early and less well-known music rarely performed in Vienna. In writing to Clara about his new position
he again referred to his unhappiness at having been slighted
in Hamburg. She answered soothingly:

> *Once more I can plainly see what a difficult position you*
> *would have had there as a native of Hamburg, and so young*
> *besides. Your wings would soon have drooped with exaspera-*
> *tion. How different things must be in Vienna!*

There were, naturally, administrative details connected
with his new position that often made Brahms impatient, such
as having to consider the wishes and differences of opinion of
the members of the choral society board concerning the programs he chose, finding the proper soloists, and often having

to change the dates of performances. All this he found frustrating, and it made him impatient.

At a second concert under his direction the Singakademie performed another Bach cantata and a large number of unaccompanied works of the 17th century. The audience found it rather a gloomy concert, and one of them, joking about Brahms's kind of program, said, "When Brahms is really merry he gets them to sing 'The Grave Is My Joy!'"

Brahms resolved that at the end of his contract he would not continue with the choral group, although he was well-liked and was asked to stay on as their conductor for three more years. He could not remain in a position that no longer interested him just for the sake of financial security. He needed more time for composing.

He decided to give only a limited number of piano lessons in order to have enough to live on; the rest of his time he would spend in composing. He was determined not to take a position, no matter how well-paying, that did not give him enough freedom to work on his own ideas. It was pleasant during this period to hear that his "Haydn Variations" had been performed in the United States by the Brooklyn Philharmonic Orchestra under Theodore Thomas, who was also conductor of the New York Philharmonic and later, in 1891, of the Chicago Symphony.

Richard Wagner, twenty years older than Brahms, was living at Penzing, a suburb of Vienna, where he rented a villa which he had had decorated according to his detailed specifications. Although Brahms had never been sympathetic to the kind of theatrical "music-drama" operas Wagner composed nor to the kind of ostentatious person he was, he appreciated Wagner's talent and respected him as a musician. When Taussig and a friend invited Brahms to go with them to Wagner's house in February 1864, he accepted gladly.

Wagner's villa was furnished on a most luxurious scale, and it seemed obvious that at the age of fifty he felt it necessary to show that he amounted to something in society. The walls of the house were festooned with silk; the lights hanging from the ceilings cast a dim radiance. The floors were covered with heavy soft carpets into which one's feet literally sank. Wagner's studio was decorated in lilac, with lilac hangings banded with dark red and gold in the corners. The dining room walls were covered by a pattern of rosebuds; the curtains were of brown wool with a Persian design; and the armchairs were of dark red plush. It was astonishing to see the maid wearing pink knee-breeches as Wagner required. Everything seemed to Brahms to be both theatrical and bizarre.

A few years before, Brahms, with three other friends, had drawn up and published an article protesting against what they felt were the false values of the "New German" school of music—"the music of the future," as Wagner and Liszt called it. The article was a protest against the arrogance of the followers of these two composers, who declared that no music of their time was worthy of more than passing interest unless it was of their own dramatic style and ideas.

Brahms's ideal had always been the exalted architecture or form of music of the great masters. Without this he felt there was only chaos, and he saw that to the "musicians of the future" form had exhausted itself.

In Brahms's work there was not only grand architecture, but also imagination. He had studied the works of great composers of the past to learn how best to master his own building material and make it into an original glowing structure, rendering the composition a living and noble experience.

At the time, Wagner was furious over Brahms's "manifesto," and had declared, "Brahms is only Mendelssohn and Schumann rolled into one." This was supposed to indicate that Brahms's music was neither new nor original. But Liszt, more of a gentleman, was generous in his attitude toward Brahms and his friends. Wagner was unsympathetic to Brahms's background, which had been entirely in the classical tradition. Bach, Beethoven, Haydn, Mozart, and Schubert represented eternal truth to Brahms. However, in Brahms this tradition became blended in a romantic exuberance of melody, with a new touch and a contribution that was entirely his own.

At Penzing Wagner asked Brahms to play something for him and he did so, playing his "Variations on a Theme of Handel." Wagner was obviously impressed by his composition and said grudgingly, "One sees that much can still be done with the old forms in the hands of one who knows how to deal with them."

In later years Brahms grew more sympathetic to Wagner's operas, for he respected Wagner's particular kind of genius. He even went to Munich to hear the first performances of the new "music-dramas." Wagner, however, became less and less generous and polite toward Brahms as the years went by and wrote vindictively of him and "his kind of music." Outside of Bach, Wagner was scornful of all classical music.

His work with the Choral Society over, Brahms returned to Hamburg for a visit, only to find the situation at home even more difficult than it had been the year before. His father, now a regular member of the Philharmonic Orchestra under Stockhausen, complained to his son that it was impossible for him to practice undisturbed at home because of Christiane's impatience with him and his music. Brahms felt that the only solution was for his father to take separate quarters where he could practice in peace. This was arranged, and Brahms's sister Elise and her mother moved to a smaller apartment. They told Brahms, "There will always be a room ready for you whenever you come to visit us." The composer's heart was heavy over the disagreements of his parents, loving them both as much as he did. From Baden-Baden, where he went to visit Clara, he wrote:

My dearest Father:

I miss news of you very much, although I cannot hope to hear anything pleasant. That Mother and Elise have reserved a room for me would please me indeed if I only thought that you would occupy it frequently! I hope that this will be the case. You can take your afternoon nap in the company of my books. Don't begrudge Mother my money; it is not important that it should last until the New Year. Money can bring a smile to many a face which would otherwise scowl.

Do your best, even if things should be unpleasant at times. Help them with the moving, and don't let yourself be driven away; the time will come when she and all the rest of us will thank you. . . .

The separation of his parents now made it necessary for Brahms to support his mother and sister entirely. As he had no fixed income it was a heavy burden to undertake. Fritz was on his own and paid no attention to any family obligations. Clara took it upon herself to write to Jakob asking him to contribute to his wife's expenses and not leave the whole burden to Johannes, but Jakob did not or could not comply, having now to pay for his own rooms and meals. From now on Brahms not only supported his mother and his sister, who earned a little from her sewing, but after his mother died he continued to send money to Elise; and later he sent money to his father when he grew too old to work.

To Brahms it was a pleasure to send them money, and if possible he sent more than he agreed to do, even urging them to spend money on luxuries. To his father he wrote:

> *Whenever you need any money, whatever the sum, you will write to me, won't you? Are you living comfortably? Do you buy as many geese as you need? If you don't, I shall send more money without being asked.*

In his own way of living, Brahms was simple and modest. Anything that went beyond normal pleasures and luxuries he called "Wagnerian"—with him a highly disapproving word.

9

A German Requiem

Clara now had a summer cottage in Lichtenthal, a suburb of Baden-Baden, the famous spa and resort, and with her were her children, Marie, twenty-three, the eldest daughter who was so devoted to her mother that she refused to marry; and Julie, the third child, now nineteen, and the prettiest of Clara's daughters. Brahms suddenly became aware of her because of her beauty and charm. When he went there during the summer he was delighted by the wooded hills where he could walk and compose, by the Black Forest with its dark pines, and by the beautiful spa itself. Because of its fame, many well-known people came there each summer, among them the Russian writer Turgenev, then forty years old. There was some discussion with Clara about having Turgenev write an opera libretto for Brahms, but finally Brahms said, "Mine will remain the fine principle of not trying an opera or a marriage."

At the spa there was also the pianist Anton Rubenstein, the "Waltz King" Johann Strauss, and Hermann Levi, the opera conductor from Karlsruhe. Levi was so impressed by Brahms as a person as well as a musician that he wrote to Clara:

> *This close contact with Johannes has had, I believe, a deep and lasting influence on my whole character, such as I cannot remember having experienced at any other period of my musical life. In him I have seen the image of a pure artist and man. . . .*

In the midst of such a group of admiring friends, and being close to Clara, compositions flowed out of Brahms more bountifully than ever. He completed the "Quintet in F Minor," developed the "Second String Sextet" and wrote a group of new songs. It was a rich harvest that summer.

Clara introduced Brahms to Princess Anna of Hesse, who was spending the summer at the resort. Having promised to play for her, Clara persuaded Brahms to go with her and play a sonata of his for two pianos that had been rearranged from his "F Minor String Quintet."

The Princess liked it so much that Brahms made her a copy and dedicated it to her. She was so delighted that she sent him as a present the original score of Mozart's *G Minor*

Symphony, the best gift possible—because to Brahms "the gods above" were Bach, Mozart, and Beethoven.

It was sad to hear, in the midst of his happiness, that his first teacher, Cossel, had died at the age of fifty-two. The bad news was offset by a letter from Joachim saying he had become a father and wanted Brahms to be godfather to his son. As Brahms could not attend the christening of Johannes Joachim, he sent as a present a charming lullaby based on an old melody, "The Virgin's Cradle Song," arranged for voice and piano with viola accompaniment.

Brahms returned to Vienna for the winter; when Christmas came and he knew he would not be home with his parents, he wrote to Jakob:

> *You must, after all, receive my greetings at Christmas. Aren't you going to spend even one evening with Mother? Doesn't Fritz do his best to persuade you to go there? I myself shall be alone, and how longingly I shall think of you!*

Among the gifts Brahms sent home was a sewing machine for his sister, who wanted and needed one for the sewing jobs she did for people. The sewing machine had just come out on the market and would be a great help to Elise, who had to do all her sewing by hand, so that she often strained her eyes and increased her headaches.

Two months later, as Brahms was playing Bach's *Goldberg Variations,* he received an urgent telegram from his brother Fritz: "If you want to see our mother once again, come immediately."

Brahms hastened home, but when he got there his mother

was dead. Completely stricken by her loss, he insisted that his father stand with him beside his mother's bed where she lay and say he forgave her. After her mother's death Elise went to live with an uncle.

Although he had never been a churchgoer, Brahms had always read the Bible, which to him contained the highest revelation of human thought and feeling; and he now resumed work on the *German Requiem*, a religious choral work which he had been planning ever since Schumann's death. It would be an expression of his grief and sorrow for his mother and for Robert Schumann.

He wrote to Clara,

There is nothing to be altered, nothing to regret for a sensible man; it's simply a matter of carrying on and keeping one's head above the waters.

Because of the additional support needed for his family in Hamburg, Brahms felt it necessary to go on a concert tour so as to supplement his meager income from teaching and the publishing of his music. In the autumn he went to Mannheim to play his "D Minor Piano Concerto" under the conductor, Levi, whom he had met the previous summer. Then he toured the important towns and cities of Switzerland. At Christmas he was in Germany and gave a concert at the court in Detmold, where he was received enthusiastically as an old friend. After that he went to Oldenburg, taking part in what became a real Brahms Festival, since most of the program consisted of his own compositions.

His summer holiday in 1866 was spent at Zürichberg, near Zürich, which had a beautiful view of the lake and mountains. There he became friends with many musicians, as well as with the eminent professor of surgery, Dr. Theodor Billroth, four years older than himself. Dr. Billroth was an accomplished pianist, could play the violin, and for a surgeon had an unusual knowledge of music. He often played duets with Brahms and when, the next year, he was made professor of surgery in Vienna, his home became the center for chamber music.

Brahms's new compositions were performed there before they were published or played publicly. Brahms often sent Billroth the score of his compositions for an opinion, arranging them for four hands and playing them as duets with Billroth if it were a big work such as a symphony, so that the doctor would understand the music better. Often large receptions and dinners were given in Dr. Billroth's beautiful home in order to introduce some new work of Brahms.

Dr. Billroth, a large plump man with an impressive head, his eyes blue, his beard blonde, was such an eloquent conversationalist that he always became the center of any group. Patients and medical men came from all over to consult him. In contrast, Brahms was lacking in company manners; but he was unselfish and generous, not only to his family but also to needy musicians and charitable musical organizations. Some people referred to Brahms as "a man of many corners" because he could bristle and he was occasionally rude and sarcastic to people of the upper classes. Despite this, Dr. Billroth was devoted to the composer and obtained so much musical joy from him that he would say of him, "art and love outlast science."

Brahms's *First Symphony* was published when he was forty-two. It was greatly influenced by Beethoven's *Ninth Symphony* and was like a struggle from darkness to light. In the finale there is kind of a jubilation, the theme like a hymn expressing its joyfulness. The beauty of the horn solo is like a beam of light when it plays:

Adagio　　　　FIRST SYMPHONY (solo for horn)

Brahms dedicated his first two string quartets, the C minor and A minor, to Dr. Billroth.

In the autumn Brahms toured Switzerland with Joachim, who was no longer at the court of Hanover because of his Archduke's abdication. Under Joachim's influence and stimulation, Brahms's piano playing took on an added beauty, and their joint concerts were so successful and such a joy to both that the next year they made another concert tour in Austria. During the eighteen months of intensive playing and composing, Brahms succeeded finally in completing the *Requiem*.

A few months after Christiane's death, Jakob had written Brahms that he had found at last a good place for his midday meal. After Christmas Brahms received another letter saying:

I am happy to sit down to write to you, but of course I never have anything to say. I have learned nothing, and lead as always a very retired life. But my home life is happy. I should like you to see it. It is as though God had sent an angel

106

*to make me forget everything. Hearty thanks, dear Johannes,
for the ten napoleons [money] with which you presented us at
Christmas; I am only sorry not to be able to send you ten
times as much.*

To Brahms's surprise still another letter arrived:

*Life, as I am now living it, contains so little that is agree-
able, it is so dull and empty, that I have decided to make a
change. I believe and hope that this will be for my happiness.
It is easily understood that I, who for thirty-four years had
lived with my family—if not always very happily—must find
it hard to accustom myself to the life I have led for the past
two years. Therefore, if you think it over, you won't hold it
against me when I tell you that I am thinking of marrying
again. My choice has fallen on a woman who, though she
won't make you forget your mother, has every right to your
respect. She suits me, and I am sure I have not made an un-
becoming choice. She is a widow, a homely body, forty-one
years of age. It would make me particularly happy if this
should be another reason for you to come here this winter. . . .
I hope, therefore, my dear Johannes, that we shall see each
other soon, and I hope until then you think kindly of my in-
tention, even if it rather surprises you. . . .*

Brahms answered with great affection:

Dearest Father:
*   When I opened your letter and found three handwritten*

pages, I looked with some trepidation for the news that caused
you to write that much. . . . Dearest Father, a thousand bless-
ings and the warmest wishes for your well-being go out to you
from here. How gladly would I sit at your side, clasp your
hand, and wish you as much happiness as you deserve, which
would be more than enough for one earthly lifetime. This step
is nothing but a handsome testimonial to yourself, and tells
us how much you have merited the happiest of family lives.

Jakob had been taking his midday meal at a boarding
house run by a widow, Frau Karoline Schnack, who had a
small son named Fritz. She was a good deal younger than
Jakob and this filled Brahms with misgivings. Worried, he decided he must go to Hamburg to meet her before his father
married her. To his surprise and pleasure he found her such
a cheerful, clever woman, and so devoted to Jakob, that he
was delighted for his father. Jakob confessed to his son that
he felt renewed and as happy as a boy because of his love for
Karoline.

For a wedding gift, Brahms sent a handsome sum of
money. He also decided that later on it would be a treat for
him and his father to have a holiday together in the mountains
of Austria. Because of several recent successful concerts he
had sufficient money for such a trip, and therefore he wrote
his father:

You are probably returning from Heide tomorrow, and
I hope that you are in such good spirits that you will immedi-
ately do what I ask you. Come to Vienna! Don't think it over

too long. Only consider that at your age, traveling becomes more difficult and less enjoyable with every year.

It goes without saying that the journey will cost you nothing, not even the loss of opportunities at Hamburg. Of course we will arrange everything so that this will not be too tiring for you. You must not and cannot deny me, and you are not to think over this offer too long. It would be best for you to start, if possible, this very night. . . . I beg you, dearest Father, kiss Mother goodbye at once, and give her a kiss for me too. Off you go! You will enjoy yourself thoroughly and you will give me the greatest pleasure. I am waiting impatiently for the announcement of your departure.

Yours,
Johannes

He sent Jakob details of train connections to Vienna and told him what things to bring with him for the trip. He could hardly wait for his father to arrive so he might introduce him to his friends. When Jakob came, Brahms's friends were charmed by his simple heartiness and good humor. After a few days the father and son left for the mountains. It was a holiday Jakob would always remember, and they enjoyed themselves together so much that they made plans to go on another trip the following summer, along the Rhine and into Switzerland.

With touching joy Brahms wrote to Joachim about the trip with his father through the Alps:

Through my father's visit and through the little trip

which we undertook together, I experienced the greatest happiness I have known in a long time. Not the least of this happiness was the enjoyment my father derived from everything new that he saw. Until then he had never seen a mountain, let alone looked down one. You can well imagine how great his astonishment was. Also it was by no means unimportant to him that he saw the Emperor twice, here with the Pasha [of Turkey], and then again in Salzburg with Napoleon [III]. Now I am again settled down and will remain here quietly; but my soul is refreshed like a body after a bath. My good father hasn't the slightest idea how much good he has done me.

After the strenuous holiday by stagecoach, mountain railway and on foot, Jakob was glad to go back to Hamburg. Brahms returned to Vienna, spending the next months getting the *German Requiem*, the memorial for his mother and Schumann, ready for performance in December. When the audience first heard it, Brahms saw that they were unmoved; but still he was not distressed, for he thought the performance had not gone well enough for them to be able to appreciate the music properly.

In April it was given again at the cathedral in Bremen with Brahms himself the conductor and Stockhausen singing the main part. Brahms had also invited four of his "dear girls" from the Ladies' Choir to sing with the Bremen chorus. Many of his best friends came to hear it, among them Clara and her eldest daughter Marie, Joachim and his wife, his father, Otto Grimm, and others. This time the *Requiem* was performed with great success, and many were moved to tears as they listened to the poignancy of the music expressing the words, "They that sow in tears shall reap in joy." It was obvious that the *Requiem* had been closer to Brahms's heart than anything he had composed in his thirty-five years.

There was a gay celebration and banquet after the performance at the Bremen Cathedral, the guests consisting of singers in the *Requiem* and his close friends. The glowing speeches and toasts for Brahms embarrassed him, and he found it difficult to say more than thanks to those who made the performance of the *Requiem* such a success.

An Englishman who was present wrote to Brahms many years later:

> *At Bremen, at the first performance of your* Requiem, *when I had the pleasure of meeting your father, I remember so well when we were coming out of the church after your great triumph that I spoke to him and asked him if he was proud of his son's triumph. But all he said was, "It was quite well done," and took a pinch of snuff. He was the only man who seemed calm. He took it for granted that his son would triumph. He remains for me the picture of a simple and strong man.*

It was not that Jakob was unmoved or unresponsive, but he was a typical North German, reserved and outwardly calm.

Because of the *Requiem's* success in Bremen, it was repeated a month later. After this Brahms added a fifth part to it, dedicating it to his mother with the words that began, "I will comfort you as a mother comforteth."

The following year the *Requiem* was performed in its final and complete five-part form more than twenty times in Germany; soon after, it was heard in London, St. Petersburg, and Paris. Because of his success with the *Requiem*, Brahms was spurred on to compose more choral works, the cantata "Rinaldo" and the beautiful "Song of the Fates," both inspired by Goethe's poetry.

The next summer, as had been arranged, Brahms and his father again had a holiday together. It gave them both much pleasure, and upon his return to Vienna Brahms decided he was tired of living in lodgings and would like a home of his own. He therefore wrote his father not to set aside a room for him in his home in Hamburg.

After all, I cannot wish to settle in Hamburg, and even if I visit you for shorter or longer periods, we can hardly for that reason keep two rooms empty all the year round. Besides, what would I do in Hamburg? Apart from you there is no one I want to see. You know well enough how little I get out of the place. In short, I realize at last that I must have some sort of home elsewhere, so I think I shall try to make myself comfortable in Vienna next autumn.

Again he received an invitation from Cologne, with even better terms, offering a teaching post at the Conservatory. In addition he would have a choir to conduct. But Brahms was not tempted. Joachim, now the director at the Royal Music College in Berlin, also asked him to come and teach there, but he refused. He felt that Vienna was more important for his musical development and happiness.

More and more sure of himself as a composer, and with a greater sense of well-being, he composed more lovely *Liebeslieder* duets, which were like delicate Viennese waltzes but containing a vocal quartet in addition to the piano parts.

During the summer of 1869, Brahms spent a few weeks with Clara in Baden-Baden. He suddenly became aware of the fact that her third daughter Julie, now twenty-three, was even lovelier than he remembered. Neither Clara nor Julie had realized his growing interest and attachment, so that when they informed him that Julie had become engaged to an Italian aristocrat, a widower with two little girls whom she met at a spa while recuperating from tuberculosis, they were astonished at the obvious shock and change in him. To a friend in Düsseldorf Clara wrote:

> *From the moment I told Johannes about Julie's engagement he became transformed, falling into a despondent mood which it took a fortnight to conquer. He is improving, but hardly speaks to Julie, whom he used to pursue with words and glances.*

A short time later Brahms sent Julie a wedding present, his "Alto Rhapsody." In her diary Clara wrote,

> *A few days ago Johannes showed me a wonderful work for contralto, male chorus, and orchestra. He called it his bridal song. It is long since I received so profound an impres-*

sion; it shook me by the deep-felt grief of its words and music. The words began, "Ah, shall any heal his anguish, whose balsam has turned to poison?"

The words were by Goethe and depicted a man filled with the agonies of loneliness and unwept tears. Clara said, "This piece can only be the manifestation of his own inward sorrow. If only once he would speak thus from the heart in words!"

But as always, Clara's problems became his, and when Brahms learned that Clara's youngest son Felix was seriously ill, he wrote her,

I feel your anxieties and sorrows much too deeply to be able to express myself about them in words. My own grief I am accustomed to bear in silence. For you I feel much more strongly and lovingly. No thought goes from me to you which does not entirely surround you and sympathize with all your cares. I love you more than myself and anyone or anything in the world.

10

A Famed Composer

At last Brahms found a place in Vienna that suited him perfectly. It was an apartment of two rooms to which he later added a third. The rooms, simply furnished, were on the third floor of a house on a quiet street, with a fine view from the windows of the Karlskirche's beautiful columns. From his rooms he could see the great square with its little bridge and a stream flowing under it. In the parlor he had his piano, his writing table, sofa, books, and a high desk at which he stood when writing his compositions.

He was now delighted to accept the position of conductor of the Friends of Music Society's orchestra. As he lived quite near to his place of work, close by the concert hall and the fine music library, he was satisfied and content. He was pleased to have, at last, a permanent home in Vienna and the kind of position he wanted. "I am in love with music," he said to a friend. "I think of nothing but music—or only of something that makes music more beautiful."

This happiness vanished when he received a letter from his stepmother telling him that his father was seriously ill. Brahms dropped everything and immediately left for Hamburg. Eleven days after his arrival, Jakob died of cancer of the liver at the age of sixty-six. Brahms was particularly sad because the last few years of his father's life had been so happy with Karoline; and with his own increased earning power he had anticipated giving his father more comforts in his old age.

His sister Elise and brother Fritz still lived in Hamburg, but Brahms felt no great bond with them, especially not with Fritz, who had been too selfish to help his parents although able to do so. Elise had worried him by marrying a widowed watchmaker, the father of six children. However, when Brahms found how happy she was with her husband and new home he was relieved and pleased. On each of her wedding anniversaries he sent her a poem for the occasion which he had written himself. Whenever he could he helped out with money, even paying for her youngest stepchild's education.

After his father's death, Brahms showed his stepmother Karoline his affection and gratitude for making his father so happy. When he returned to Vienna after Jakob's funeral, he wrote her on March 4, 1872:

My dear Mother:

*Many times I have begun to write to you. I thought of
you, indeed, most affectionately. I thought further and further
back into the past—but it couldn't be put into writing. Neither
that, nor words of consolation. And even now I can't attempt
to console you. I know too well what we have both lost, and
how lonely your life has become. I hope, however, that now
you are doubly conscious of the love of others—and finally,
of my own love, which is entirely and wholly yours. I have
received so many marks of sympathy here that you would
have been happy to see how Father was valued by all who
knew him. I am sending you 1,000 thalers. You can give Elise
her share of that.*

*May I ask you to write in good time when and how much
money I shall send? Simply tell me the sum you need. Now
my most heartfelt greetings and as you assuredly know how
I loved my father, so, too, be sure that I shall always, and for
all time, in truest and most grateful love, be*

Yours,

Johannes

Although he found it a burden to write letters, Brahms
often sent Karoline money, presents, and reviews of his concerts. He also wrote to her son Fritz Schnack ("the other Fritz,"
as Jakob had called him) and bought him a watch and clock-
maker's business in another town when he reached adulthood.

Brahms was thirty-nine when he started his work as con-

118

ductor for the Friends of Music Society. He was also to be director of Vienna's leading choral group. The first thing he felt he had to do was strengthen the orchestra by weeding out the weaker members and replacing them with better ones obtained from the Court Opera Orchestra. Then he decided to have two weekly rehearsals of the choir instead of one as they had had before. His choral programs consisted of Bach, Handel, Mozart, and 17th-century works, for he was greatly interested in early music and had developed a deep understanding of its style and performance. He rarely played his own compositions except when strongly urged.

His concerts were highly successful, although his programs were thought too serious; and Brahms himself was greatly appreciated. But at the end of his three-year term he decided to give up the position because, as before, he found that his many duties did not give him enough time to compose. That summer of 1873 he went to Tützing, near Munich. There he became acquainted with the Munich musical circle and made many new friends. While there he completed two string quartets, one of which he dedicated to Dr. Billroth, and he also wrote the "Variations on a Theme of Haydn" in two versions, one for orchestra and one for two pianos. He also composed what amounted to almost a whole volume of songs, stimulated and inspired by the beautiful surroundings of the simple village and the kindly Tützing country folk.

In September there was to be a Schumann Festival in Bonn for the benefit of a monument to Schumann. Joachim would be leader of the festival, and the committee asked Brahms to compose a special work for the occasion. However, he refused because he could not find a suitable text for such a composition, whereupon Joachim suggested that the *German Requiem* be performed. The committee did not agree to this because it would require more musicians and singers than they could assemble; and because Brahms was so modest in saying it did not matter whether a work of his was performed or not, Joachim decided to do no more about it. Consequently there was no work of Brahms's on the program.

But somehow Brahms had received the impression that the *Requiem* was going to be performed; so when he learned from the newspaper that nothing of his was on the program he was terribly hurt and upset. He blamed Joachim and Clara, in charge of the program, for his being slighted. He did attend the festival, trying to hide his disappointment; but his chagrin was obvious.

Despite his temporary resentment, Brahms still considered Joachim and Clara to be his best friends; when he wrote to Clara later he ended the letter saying, "I love you more than myself and more than anybody or anything on earth."

To Grimm he wrote afterwards:

To me, Schumann's memory is sacred. This noble, pure artist forever remains my ideal. I will hardly be privileged ever to love a person better. Neither, it is to be hoped, will I have to come again so horrifyingly close to such a dreadful fate and share such suffering.

In the summer he again went to Switzerland for his holiday and to compose. He wrote his "Vocal Quartets" and some

120

new *Liebeslieder*. Schubert's dances were the inspiration for the *"Liebeslieder* Waltzes" which quickly became popular. However, Brahms's waltzes were vocal and meant as music to be sung at home among one's family. Brahms enjoyed being by the shores of Lake Zurich, and his new songs reflected this pleasure.

The following summer he lived near Heidelberg where he completed more duets and rewrote a piano quartet. He was relieved to be rid of his demanding position in Vienna, and realized more than ever that he should never undertake another.

His fame grew to such a degree that he began receiving invitations from many countries to give concerts and conduct his compositions; but he had made up his mind never to spend more than three months of the year on activities outside of composing. He wished to spend autumn, winter, and spring in Vienna, then early in the summer set out for some pretty place in the country to think out and complete new compositions.

In 1876 he went on a concert tour to Holland, where he had so many friends and admirers that it became almost an annual event for him to go there. Among his friends was the eminent physician and physiologist, Dr. Theodor Engelmann of Utrecht, ten years younger than Brahms. They had first met in Switzerland in 1866 when Brahms was thirty-three. Because of Dr. Engelmann's interest in music a bond was established between them. Later they met again in Germany when Brahms played some of his most recent compositions.

Brahms was pressed to come to England to play the next

year and was offered an honorary degree at Cambridge University; but he could not bring himself to go there even though Joachim was to receive a musical doctorate at the same time. It was partly because he disliked crossing the sea and partly because he spoke English badly and hated ceremonies of any kind. Musicians and critics wrote begging him to come, for he was required to accept the honor in person, and one of them said, "London does not take second place to any city in its admiration of you."

Brahms wrote to Stanford, the composer and professor of music at Cambridge University, saying why he could not come to receive the honorary degree:

My dear and honored Sir:

I find it difficult to take pen in hand, for how can I speak of my deep gratitude and yet say no? And still I am earnestly and sincerely thankful to you for your graciousness and to your university for the great honor which it wishes to bestow upon me. But by next July the answer will still have to be no, even though today I would rather keep it from you as well as from myself and talk myself out of it. But please think of this: I cannot go to Cambridge without also going to London, and in London there is a great deal to see and to do—all this in beautiful midsummer when you also would undoubtedly prefer to take a walk with me along one of the lovely Italian lakes.

I am certainly tempted to accept your invitation. Will it not be a very special kind of musical celebration? And would I not run the risk of being outdone and put to shame, as far as youthfulness and gratitude are concerned, by old man Verdi? [Verdi was then twenty years older than Brahms.] But even if today I were to follow my desires and promise to come, I know only too well that when the time arrived, I would not possibly be able to make up my mind to undertake the trip and all that is inevitably connected with it.

When he also received an invitation to become music director of the orchestra in Düsseldorf, Brahms refused to leave Vienna. He wrote about it to Dr. Billroth on October 17, 1876:

Dear Friend:

You will have learned through Feber that there has been a request for me to come to Düsseldorf. I have long wished for such a position, and I must turn a very serious face to this affair. I do not like to go away from Vienna, and I have a good deal against Düsseldorf. Of course, finances also have a word to say! If I accepted I'd have to be there in January. My chief objections to accepting are also of a childish nature. . . . Perhaps they include the good restaurants and winehouses in Vienna and the, to me, disagreeable and rough atmosphere of Düsseldorf. In Vienna one can be a bachelor without any more discussion. But in a little city, an old bachelor is a caricature. I will not marry, and have some grounds left to be still a little frightened by the fair sex.

Heartily yours,
J. Brahms

In 1877, Brahms composed for Clara an ingenious arrangement for left hand alone of Bach's "Chaconne for Solo Violin" from one of the suites for unaccompanied violin; he sent it to her with a letter:

Dear Clara:

I think it is a long time since I sent anything so amusing, providing your fingers survive the pleasure. The chaconne is one of the most marvelous and incomprehensible musical forms that exists. This man [Bach] is capable of writing for a small instrument a whole world of deep thoughts. He translates the most powerful sensations. Could I have imagined conceiving or writing such a piece I think I should have gone mad with excitement and bewilderment.

Clara was delighted with this brilliant showpiece and said she found it "wonderful."

In the summer he went to the island of Rügen in the Baltic off the coast of north Germany with a friend, George Henschel, who was a singer and who became the first conductor of the Boston Symphony Orchestra, and later of the London Symphony Concerts.

While in Rügen with Brahms, Henschel one day began whistling the Andante from Brahms's "C Minor Piano Quartet." Brahms was pleased, then said, "Can you imagine how those gods Mozart, Beethoven, and the other great ones must have felt when they put the finishing touch to masterpieces like *The Marriage of Figaro* and the *Ninth Symphony*? What I don't understand is how men like myself can be vain. To tell you the truth—when people praise me to the skies, I should

124

be disgusted if it weren't so ridiculous."

In Rügen Brahms completed his *First Symphony* which he had begun fourteen years earlier, and which he himself described to his publisher as "lovely."

Brahms could hardly wait to hear how it sounded. It is a symphony full of a grandeur and tenderness that reflects the inspiring country places where he spent his summers. It was conducted in Karlsruhe by Levi, who had become Brahms's good friend. It met with a good deal of success, and so there were also performances in Munich, Vienna, Leipzig, Breslau, London, Cambridge, and other cities.

Because Brahms had dedicated his first and second string quartets to Dr. Billroth, and the third to Dr. Engelmann of Utrecht, Dr. Billroth, who knew Engelmann, wrote him:

I'm afraid these dedications will keep our names longer in the public memory than the best medical work we've done. For us, this is not very complimentary; but it is beautiful for humanity, which with the right instinct considers art more immortal than science.

11

One of the Three B's

Brahms spent the following summer in Austria in the lovely village of Portschach, where he composed his *Second Symphony in D Major*. He wrote a friend that the air was so full of flying melodies that he had to take good care not to step on them.

Full of mischief, he wrote to his publisher Simrock about it and said, "The new symphony is so melancholy [which it was not, but rather one of his gayest and happiest works] that you will not be able to put up with it. Never before have I penned anything so sorrowful, so *minor*. The score must be published with a black border. Don't say I haven't warned you. Do you really think you should invest in such a thing?"

When Dr. Billroth played it on the piano for the first time he declared: "It is all rippling streams, sky, sunshine, and cool green shadows. How beautiful it must be at Portschach!"

The beauty of the *Second Symphony,* the charm of the "Violin Concerto," dedicated to Joachim, and the tenderness of the "G Major Violin Sonata" sprang from Brahms's three happy productive summers in Portschach. At this stage of his life his symphonies, which he composed in pairs, were the summit of his creative talent. The symphonies are as often performed today as in the past and are completely different in character, style, and effect. They are so full of melody that one could sing each movement from beginning to end, as if it were a single uninterrupted song.

The first performance of the *Second Symphony* in Vienna in December 1877 was such a success that the delightful third movement had to be played over again. Even the cold audiences of Hamburg rejoiced over this work. When the Hamburg Philharmonic Orchestra was celebrating its fiftieth anniversary with a music festival, all the leading musicians were invited including Clara, Joachim and Brahms. His symphony would be performed there, with Joachim the concertmaster and Brahms the conductor. Many of the orchestra musicians were Brahms's old friends. The *Second Symphony* was a sensation, and Brahms was given a laurel wreath and showered with roses. It was some solace for his not having been recognized there earlier and given the post of conductor of the Hamburg orches-

tra when he had so much wished to have it. Now all the important Hamburg citizens vied with each other to honor Brahms, their distinguished native son.

The summer in the southern province of Austria called Carinthia was once again a fruitful time for Brahms. He composed his first motet, the "Ballads for Piano," and a great many lovely songs. During the next summers there he composed capriccios, intermezzos, and rhapsodies, all for piano, and his "First Violin Sonata," full of melody and tenderness. This crowning work was intended for Joachim to play. On New Year's day, 1879, Joachim performed it in Leipzig, but it was more warmly received in England than it was in Europe.

Brahms's free and beautiful summers, when he roamed in the woods and along the streams as Beethoven had done, thinking and preparing his compositions in his mind, always bore good results. His musical thoughts and ideas were more abundant and clear when he could be outdoors in the midst of nature, among inspiring surroundings. Beethoven had found the same kind of inspiration in nature. Brahms's vitality as a person and composer was constantly increasing, and ideas for his works flowed freely, rushing along and overcoming all obstacles like a mighty river.

Dr. Theodor Billroth continued to be a devoted friend, and Brahms often shared with Clara the many interesting letters he received from the surgeon-musician, giving his opinion about Brahms's new works. Billroth's approval and praise were important to Brahms.

Busy as he was and preoccupied with his compositions, Brahms was never too busy to help a young musician or composer. He would try to get them recognized, have their works published, find money to tide them along. So it was with the Czech composer Antonin Dvořák, when he first came to Vienna as a young man. Not only did Brahms get him a state scholarship, but he also found a conductor to perform his compositions. He persuaded Simrock, his publisher, to bring out some of Dvořák's works and he offered him financial help. Dvořák's traditional Slavonic manner of expression in his music delighted Brahms. On one occasion Brahms even corrected proofs of Dvořák's music before they went to press, when Dvořák was absent in New York as music director of the National Conservatory. It was due to his being in the United States that he composed the New World Symphony. Dvořák wrote in gratitude to his friend:

> *Your warm encouragement and the pleasure you seem to find in my work have moved me deeply and made me unspeakably happy. I can hardly tell you, Esteemed Master, all that is in my heart. I can only say that I shall all my life owe you the deepest gratitude for your good and noble intentions toward me, which are worthy of a truly great artist and man.*
>
>

Your ever grateful
Antonin Dvořák

For a long time Brahms had had a great desire to visit Italy. He finally made plans to go there in the spring of 1878 with Dr. Billroth, who was a connoisseur of art and would be an excellent companion, having been there many times before. The winter before the trip, Brahms studied guide books and maps, and he could hardly wait for spring to arrive. They saw Milan, Rome, Siena, Florence, Venice, and Naples. Brahms fell so deeply in love with Italy that he decided to stay on in that lovely country to celebrate his forty-fifth birthday on May 7th.

While in Italy, one of his great pleasures was to hunt for old engravings in various antique shops; when he found something he wanted he was as elated as a little boy. He knew how to enjoy life and even small pleasures did not leave him unmoved. He wrote to Clara:

> *How often do I not think of you and wish that you might know the delight which the eye and heart experience here! If you stood for only one hour in front of the façade of the Cathedral of Siena, you would be overjoyed, and would agree that this alone made the journey worthwhile. And, on entering, you would find at your feet and throughout the church no single corner that did not give you the same joy. On the following day, in Orvieto, you would be forced to acknowledge that the cathedral there was even more beautiful. And after all this, to plunge into Rome is a delight beyond all words. . . .*
>
> *We have still the best time of the year before us, and one has only to take a little trouble to enjoy it in comfort. Next year you must see that you are free at the end of March, when I shall be able to be with you on the whole of the journey—by that time I shall have become a thorough Italian, and shall be able to be of use to you.*

Everything about Italy, excepting Italian music, enchanted Brahms and made him feel joyful and gay.

When he returned to Vienna he was wearing a beard which he had grown during the summer. His friends did not recognize him, for it made him look so much older; many were amused or shocked by his different appearance. Brahms enjoyed the transformation and thought the beard gave him dignity and grandeur—and besides, he wouldn't have to wear a necktie under it. No one would know the difference!

In the autumn of 1879, Brahms and Joachim made a concert tour through Hungary. There in Budapest they met Liszt and the French composer Berlioz and visited cordially. After that they went to Poland, and then played in cities along the Rhine in Germany. It was a strenuous concert tour, but Brahms felt it had been worthwhile and rewarding.

The next year, in May, he was invited to be the conductor of a concert to be given during the unveiling of the monument for Schumann. In the summer he went to the Austrian spa, Ischl, where many of the nobility and famous musicians came. Among them he again met Johann Strauss, who had a beautiful house and gave fancy parties. Brahms was often invited there but he was not always as polite as he should have been, unable to be patient with pretentious society people.

During the summer he composed the lively and humorous "Academic Festival Overture" for the honorary degree awarded him by the University of Breslau. The exuberant "Overture," in which one can almost imagine beer tankards raised, was based on some popular student songs and was stirring and tuneful. The "Tragic Overture," composed that same summer, was an entirely different kind of music; it was serious and sad. Clara called it "magnificent" because it was so full of compassion.

Unfortunately his devoted friendship of thirty years with Joachim suddenly cooled. It came about because Joachim was having marital difficulties and Brahms gallantly took Frau Joachim's part. Joachim felt Brahms had been unfair and disloyal, and when Amalie divorced him, he broke off the friendship with Brahms entirely, although he continued to play Brahms's works with his usual devotion. Joachim said, "Whoever writes like this must be noble and good."

Brahms, sad at losing Joachim's friendship, still had the friendship of Hans von Bülow, the extraordinary pianist and conductor who had been an ardent disciple of Wagner's until Bülow's wife Cosima, Liszt's daughter, left him to marry Wagner. Bülow had conducted Brahms's *First Symphony* in Hanover a few years before, and in his enthusiasm referred to it then as "The Tenth," as if to proclaim it the first successor to Beethoven's nine symphonies. At present he was music director of the orchestra at the cultivated court of Meiningen. The concerts he gave with his well-trained orchestra were considered remarkable.

In Ischl, during the summer of 1881, Brahms completed a new work, the "Second Piano Concerto in B♭ Major," his favorite key. The composition had been greatly influenced by his happy impressions of Italy, filled with recollected serenity and ethereal moods. When he sent it to his publisher and was paid for it he wrote, "Here is the receipt for my heart's blood. Also my thanks for the purchase price of a poor little piece of soul."

Bülow performed the concerto at the court of Meiningen with Brahms at the piano, and on this festive occasion Duke George and his wife conferred the Grand Cross on Brahms as a special honor. Brahms liked the Duke and his wife and always enjoyed staying at their palace, no longer feeling oppressed by luxury and formality. Brahms enjoyed the remarkable plays given at the Duke's famous theatre, as well as the music, and he often performed for the Duke and his friends. Because of this friendship, Brahms dedicated his "Song of the Fates," composed in 1882, to him.

This lyrical piano concerto was composed three years after his violin concerto and twenty-two years after his "First Piano Concerto." It is full of a great calmness and rich imagination. In the opening horn melody there is a sense of deep thought and inspiration. It is the most meaningful of all his piano concertos.

FIRST PIANO CONCERTO (melody for horn)

All in all, though, honors meant little to Brahms; he would say, "When a nice melody comes to my mind I prefer it to the Leopold Medal, and if it should make the writing of a symphony possible I would prefer it even to being given the keys of the city."

During the months Brahms was in Vienna he enjoyed taking walks in the Prater, the great public park and amusement center. He still liked to visit the restaurants and amusement booths, see the acrobats and watch the children on the merry-go-round, especially in the spring when the trees were in bloom. His pockets were always full of pennies and candies for the children he met on the way. Many of them already knew him because of his playfulness and friendly manner.

So delighted was Bülow with Brahms and his lovely compositions that he began lavishing on him all the devotion he had formerly given to Wagner, who had stolen his wife. He rehearsed a great many of Brahms's compositions with his orchestra, for they planned to go on tour and he wanted them heard and appreciated properly. It was Bülow who coined the phrase, "the three B's—Bach, Beethoven, and Brahms." Bülow truly believed that after Bach and Beethoven Brahms was the greatest composer; he claimed that Brahms's music always restored him to health of body and mind.

The following summer Brahms decided to go to Wiesbaden in Germany because a singer, Hermine Spies, a talented pupil of Stockhausen, was there. He had heard her sing his "Song of the Fates" and was greatly taken by her beautiful contralto voice and by the fact that she was a young, vivacious, pretty girl from the Rhineland. He thought the way she sang his songs was just the way he intended them to sound and because of this he grew fond of her.

He liked to tease her and make sarcastic remarks, but she, in her spirited way, returned his teasing in full measure, which delighted Brahms.

She became his favorite interpreter of the "Alto Rhapsody," and he followed her career with great interest. To help her career, he gave her letters of introduction to people in the musical circles of Vienna and often sent her songs before they were published. There were many who thought Brahms was in love with Hermine because he was so exceptionally lively and gay when he was with her. Years later she said, "What a dear he was! He is eternally young."

Brahms was about fifty then, and the young Hermine considered him to be rather elderly. Up to now he had already composed about one hundred and fifty songs for solo voice and piano accompaniment, to say nothing of vocal duets with piano, songs for mixed voices with and without orchestra, and choruses for women's voices.

❦ 12 ❧

The Old Bachelor

After Brahms had sent Clara a copy of his *Third Symphony*, she wrote him from Frankfurt:

> *I do not know where these lines will reach you, but I have to send them to you for my heart is overflowing. Thanks to your marvellous symphony [Symphony No. 3 in F Major] I have spent many pleasant hours. I have played it over several times on the piano with Elise and I simply have to let you know.*

What a work! What lyricism! There is such harmony throughout, each movement is like a limpid spring, a heartbeat, a treasure. From beginning to end it evokes the secret life of forests. I cannot tell you which movement I prefer. In the first I am dazzled by the brilliance of awakening dawn, the rays of light trickling through the trees. Everything springs to life. Everything breathes joy. It is a delight!

The second movement is a pure idyll. I can hear the worshippers praying in the little wayside shrine and the buzzing of the bees. One feels completely inebriated by the luxuriance of nature.

The third is a pearl, a grey pearl like a sad tear. And at the end the modulation is miraculous. And that throb of passion in the last movement! The heart is on fire, but soon it calms itself for the final transfiguration, the admirable developmental motif which begins with such exceptional beauty that words fail me.

Now that I know the symphony well, I am miserable because I cannot hear it played by an orchestra.

I think of you.

Your

Clara

His love of Clara had brought out some of his best compositions; she had become the recognized interpreter of his works and he valued her judgment. He shared with this spiritually loved woman all the happy and sad events connected with her and her children, as well as anything that happened in his own life.

138

Because of the *Third Symphony*, Brahms had the excuse of renewing his friendship with Joachim by writing to ask him if he would be interested in performing it in Berlin, where Joachim was now conductor of the city orchestra. Joachim was too fine a person to let his personal feelings interfere in what he considered to be an important musical matter, and he gladly agreed. The symphony had been first performed in Vienna under the conductor Rocheter, Brahms's friend. The result was a fierce attack by the followers of Wagner who were hostile mainly because of Brahms's increasing fame. On the whole, however, the Viennese public did like the symphony, and in Berlin, under Joachim, it was so successful that it was performed three times in succession. At Meiningen, Bülow conducted it and performed it twice at the very same concert because the audience liked it so much.

Once again Brahms was approached to become the conductor of the Cologne Municipal Orchestra, this time at a huge salary and with all kinds of inducements. But Brahms refused and wrote:

> *How I formerly used to long for such employment, which is not only desirable but even essential for the creative artist to enable him to lead a decent and fitting existence. I am thinking now of Hamburg, my native city, where, since the time when I think I began to amount to something, my name has been repeatedly ignored.*

The next summer he went to Murzzuschlag, a little town in the Austrian province of Styria. Clara and some other friends came to see him there and found him busily at work on his *Fourth Symphony*. He went to the same village the following summer of 1885 to complete it. Now he could hardly wait for Bülow to try it out with his orchestra in Meiningen before it was performed elsewhere. The orchestra, inspired by it, played magnificently. Soon after, the orchestra went on tour with it, Brahms coming along as the second conductor with Bülow.

Joachim was absolutely delighted by the new symphony and it became his favorite of Brahms's four symphonies. He conducted it so superbly that Brahms wrote him:

> *Praise and sympathy such as yours are not only highly gratifying, but necessary. It is as though one had to wait for them for permission to enjoy one's own work.*

Now that the break in their friendship was healing, Brahms again began asking Joachim for his opinion and help about technical matters in his compositions. Joachim had always been Brahms's favorite adviser, especially when he was younger, and he greatly valued his criticism. Self-critical himself, Brahms nevertheless liked suggestions on how to improve a composition from those whose opinion he respected. In the end, however, he would decide for himself, as seen in a letter he wrote to Joachim about his "Double Concerto."

> *Now, when you see our concerto in print, please do not consider it utterly deceitful if at times I urgently requested your opinion, and then ended up by letting my own ideas stand anyway. . . .*

140

The Baroness, wife of the duke at Meiningen, invited him repeatedly to spend the summer at one of their ducal estates in Berchtesgaden; but Brahms, who feared for his independence, wrote her in 1887:

I imagine you must often consider me ungrateful or even disloyal, and in a certain sense you are justified. It is only that when I am offered the benefits of your great and bountiful generosity and kindness, often I must renounce them. I need complete solitude, not only to achieve my best work, but even to think of my work at all. This is part of my nature. We "little ones" must learn at an early age that we have to renounce things, even with a heavy heart. But now, with a new and larger composition [the "Double Concerto" for violin and cello] before me, I can take a little pride in myself and say: "I would never have written it if I had enjoyed life, no matter how much, on the Rhine or in Berchtesgaden!"

The next summer Brahms was again in Switzerland, at Thun near Berne. He enjoyed the magnificent views of lake and mountains, and there he composed two more violin sonatas, the "Concerto for Violin and Cello," the "Second Cello Sonata," a "Trio in C Minor," the eleven "Gypsy Songs" and others. What changed least in style from the beginning to the end of his life were his songs, which were jewels of lyricism. No matter how complicated or simple the accompaniment, the vocal part always remained a sweet, folk-like melody.

Widmann, a poet friend of Brahms who lived in Berne and saw him often, described him at this time:

141

Wide awake at the first break of dawn, he brewed his first breakfast on his Viennese coffee machine. A faithful lady admirer from Marseilles sent him excellent mocha for it, and in such abundance that from the very beginning he was able to share it with my household. The morning hours were devoted to work. In his quarters in Thun, where a large arbor and a lodging of several spacious rooms permitted him to walk about pensively and undisturbed by anyone, he labored particularly well. For his noon meals Brahms went to some outdoor restaurant whenever the weather permitted.

He did not like to dress up and felt most comfortable in a striped wool shirt without a collar and without a necktie. Even his soft felt hat was more often carried in his hand than worn on his head.

When on Saturday of each week he came to Berne to spend the weekend with me, usually staying until Tuesday or Wednesday, he would carry a leather traveling case. This resembled an itinerant mineralogist's specimen bag filled with rocks, but mostly contained the books I had lent him the previous week, which he brought back to be exchanged for others. In bad weather an old, brownish-gray plaid, held together in front by an enormous pin, hung over his shoulders and completed his queer, unstylish appearance, causing people to stare at him in astonishment.

Often Widmann joked with Brahms about still being a bachelor, and he replied:

I missed my chance. When I still had the urge I was

*unable to offer a woman what would have been necessary.
At the time when I was still willing to get married, my compositions were received with hisses or with cold silence. I myself
was perfectly able to put up with this, because I knew exactly
what they were worth, and that the picture would eventually
change. When I would return alone to my lodgings, I was by
no means discouraged. On the contrary! But if at such mo-
ments I had had to face a wife, her questioning eyes anxiously
seeking mine, only to tell her that again it was nothing—that
I could not have endured. For no matter how much a woman
may love the artist who is her husband and, as the saying
goes, have faith in him, she can never know the full certainty
of eventual victory that lives in his breast. And if she had
tried to console me—a woman's commiseration for her husband's failure—bah! I can't bear to think what a hell on earth
that would have been, at least the way I feel about it!*

Brahms continually worried about Clara, still straining
herself with concerts and teaching when she was already well
on in her sixties and not as vigorous as before. He wrote her
on July 24, 1888:

*I am counting on your goodness and the affection you
have for me to be granted a favor.*

*You know that I take a great interest in everything con-
cerning you, in the troubles and sorrows from which a life as
full as yours cannot possibly be exempt. I do not take small
financial troubles very seriously, but it annoys me to think
that you have any worries while I am wallowing in money*

143

which brings me no pleasure.

I cannot and do not want to live in any other way. My family receive more from me than they really need, and I can easily help others without being embarrassed in the slightest.

As for what happens after my death, I have no obligations and no particular wishes.

In short the situation is quite simple!

I have been thinking about it recently and wonder whether I could send you a small amount of money as though it were from a rich, anonymous patron of the arts, or whether I should make a belated contribution to the Schumann Fund?

Whom could I turn to for advice? The affair, I repeat, is quite simple, and you should allow me to help with your expenses and to send you 10,000 marks.

My publisher, Simrock, has taken a number of chorales, quartets, and songs. I never notice the fine royalties he pays into the Reichsbank, which lie there untouched and useless.

Now think of the pleasure you would give me if you said "Yes."

Just send me a nice postcard with a happy "Yes."

Your

Johannes

Clara, at Franzenbad that summer, wrote him gratefully:

I could not help being deeply touched. Words are nothing compared with what I feel. I can only clasp your hand affectionately and say that your offer brought me a sense of relief such as I have not felt for some time. But I cannot accept your offer at this time, because I have no motive for doing so.

Touring England last year and this year have brought me sufficient money. . . . Things are all right with me at the moment and I am not obliged to touch my capital.

I have come to the following conclusion: I look upon you as the very kind friend you are and I love you enough to promise that I will approach you without hesitation if I really have any serious difficulties. I hope you know you can believe my promises. I beg you to do nothing for the moment.

Your old true
Clara

{13}

The Music's Ending

Before Brahms returned from Thun his landlady, who was also his housekeeper, died. This presented a problem. Frau Fellinger, a friend of his, arranged that he give the former landlady's rooms, which he now took over, to the widow of a literary man and her two little boys in exchange for looking after him and his own rooms. Brahms was delighted with the arrangement and particularly enjoyed the two "darling boys." His great pleasure was to set up a fir tree for them in his library at Christmas and give them Christmas presents. He now added a few

146

more small comforts to his simple rooms which his new house-keeper, Frau Truxa, took care of. She mended his clothes and kept him neat. But she sighed with dismay as she saw one pair of his trousers, cut off by him with scissors high above his shoes. He could not get a tailor to make the trousers short enough.

His days now took on a regular pattern. He rose early, made his own coffee and light breakfast, then spent the morning at work. Usually he took lunch and supper at the Red Hedgehog, an inn where many of the musical Viennese gathered. There he enjoyed the good food and wine and could visit with his friends. In the afternoon he worked, and after supper he again went to the inn to have his last cup of coffee.

When he was informed that his old friend Dr. Billroth was extremely ill with pneumonia he was greatly distressed, although of late they had become rather distant from each other. Brahms had happened to see a letter written by Dr. Billroth to a mutual friend mentioning Brahms's rudeness and his lack of manners at times, and casting aspersions on his poor education and neglected upbringing. Brahms was terribly wounded and angered by the criticism, especially since he was so devoted to the memory of his parents. He had already forgotten that one evening not long ago as he was leaving a party at Dr. Billroth's home he had turned at the door and said gruffly to everyone present, "If there is anyone here whom I have not insulted this evening, I beg his pardon!"

It was because of this incident that Dr. Billroth told a friend, "Brahms really makes it very difficult for one to keep on loving him."

Dr. Billroth and Brahms had tried to hide their hurt from each other, but it had gone deep and needed more time to heal. Brahms no longer went to Billroth's home nor sent him his music. Brahms transferred his affections to young musicians and composers whom he could help, and they found in him not only a man of great genius but one of rare kindliness, too, who showed not only a deep interest in their careers but also in their personal and domestic lives.

Brahms decided not to go on any more concert tours. He did not care to travel much, since he was happy in Austria and also since he did not have enough time to practice sufficiently. He no longer felt at ease before an audience. No matter how relaxed the performer looked, the inner strain was great; whatever playing he would do from now on would be among his own friends. He went to Meiningen to hear splendid performances of Bach, Mozart, and his own works. To Ischl, within easy reach of Vienna, he returned again and again. It became his favorite summer place. He liked the beautiful scenery there and enjoyed the warm-hearted, gay inhabitants who protested if he didn't come when they expected him.

While at Ischl, in the summer of 1889, he received the Leopold Order from the Austrian Emperor to honor him for his distinguished contributions to music. And from the Burgomaster of Hamburg came a telegram saying:

I am happy to inform you that the "Honorary Freedom of Hamburg" has been conferred on you.

This was considered a great honor. Up to that time only twelve people, among them Bismarck, had received the Honorary Freedom of the city of Hamburg. Although Brahms was pleased, he could not help thinking somewhat bitterly that it was a little late to be honored as a citizen of Hamburg, since they had never given him the opportunity of remaining in that city by offering him a permanent position.

The next summer, while again at Ischl, he completed his "String Quintet in G Major," Opus 111, which is the peak of his inspired chamber music. With that Brahms began to feel that he had exhausted his creative powers. He considered that he was old at fifty-seven and should retire. "I have worked enough," he said. "Now let the young folks take over." He decided to destroy all of his compositions which he considered unworthy of publication, to make sure none of these would be issued after his death. He looked over those he found good enough to develop further and began thinking of how to dispose of his possessions after his death. He told friends, "There is no real creation without hard work. That which you would call invention—that is to say, a thought, an idea—is simply an inspiration for which I am not responsible, and owes no merit to me. It is a present, a gift, which I ought even to despise until I have made it my own through hard work. And there need be no hurry about that, either. It is like a seed: it germinates unconsciously and in spite of ourselves."

Because he thought that the "musicians of the future" were giving up the traditional form of music, which Brahms considered the basis of good music, he continued to be impatient with them.

He began making provision for gifts to charitable musical

societies; to the Friends of Music Society he would leave some money, his music books, and his large collection of valuable original manuscripts. These consisted of an unpublished work of Schubert, a quartet of Haydn's, Mozart's *G Minor Symphony,* sixteen pages of Beethoven's *Sketch Books,* songs by Schumann, the first sketch of Schumann's *B Minor Symphony,* manuscripts by Cherubini, Frescobaldi, Handel, Orlando di Lasso, Palestrina, the collected editions of Beethoven, Mozart, Schubert, Bach, Handel, Schütz, Chopin, Bizet, scores of some of Wagner's operas, and works by Dvořák, Strauss, and others.

The handwriting of the great masters in letters and musical scores had always excited Brahms. He once wrote to a friend: "Yesterday I bought the manuscripts of six Haydn quartets! Would you not also have a feeling of some emotion if you held something like this in your hands and called it your own?"

He set aside sums for his sister Elise, for his stepmother, for his housekeeper, Frau Truxa, and for his landlord in Ischl who had been so friendly and kind to him; but nothing for Fritz, who had already died.

Two months after making out his will, thinking he would produce no further creative work, to his own surprise and joy he unexpectedly felt a fresh burst of energy. It was due to the beautiful clarinet playing of Richard Mühlfeld in the Meiningen orchestra. Hearing and meeting him at the Meiningen court in 1891 inspired Brahms to compose for him a "Clarinet Trio," and then a "Clarinet Quintet," considered one of the loveliest pieces of chamber music ever written. The first theme of the opening movement begins:

CLARINET QUINTET (opening movement)

These two works were performed by Mühlfeld in Berlin in December, with the Joachim Quartet playing the string parts. The serene and tender music was such a huge success that Brahms's inspiration in composing them was called a "sublime vision." The importance of Brahms's clarinet works for clarinetists cannot be overestimated. They are played again and again by clarinetists in public and at home, and there are few clarinet compositions to equal them.

Clara, now seventy-two years old and ailing, did not see Brahms as often as before, and she often felt that he was neglecting her because of his closer friendship with others. Previously he had always turned to her for her opinion of each new composition, sharing with her his triumphs and disappointments. Now he began receiving bitter letters from her. Feeling that their friendship was at stake, he decided that on her birthday he would prove to her that she was wrong about him. From Vienna he wrote:

> *There are no more delightful people or children anywhere. I never go out without a joyful heart, nor without a sensation of having had a refreshing drink when I pat a few of the darling children on the head. I am solemn enough at home and am glad to see a friendly face when I go out. And now I think of yours, the friendliest and most beloved of all, and send greetings with all my heart.*

151

In the next year, on May 7, 1893, Brahms would be sixty. Knowing that there would be many festivities to honor him and disliking ceremonies of any kind, he decided to escape them by going to Italy and Sicily with two friends, one of them a Swiss conductor, the other a Hungarian pianist. While there he received many telegrams of congratulation and he learned that the Friends of Music Society were having a Brahms Medal made in his honor, one in gold for him, and fifty in bronze for him to give friends. This pleased Brahms very much, and he made out a list of the people who should receive the bronze ones, among them Hanslick, the music critic.

Hanslick wrote in his memoirs about Brahms:

Brahms is an entirely self-reliant character who, although revered and beloved by many, seems to need no one for his own heart's satisfaction. Whatever was harsh or at times even crude was softened by the flowery breath of the Austrian landscape and by the sunny smile of fortune and renown. He who cannot put up with the slightest abridgment of his personal freedom might not have become the happiest of husbands but would definitely have been a most affectionate father. Nowhere was there any little child who did not run toward the stocky graybeard, or who did not wave at him from afar. In addition to his good humor, it is his robust health which constantly gives me renewed joy. He has already passed his sixtieth birthday, and yet he has never known the slightest sickness in all his life. He still goes on walking tours like a young student, and he sleeps like a baby.

Brahms now composed more piano pieces and added accompaniments to additional German folk songs that he had been collecting over the years and which were his favorites. As he prepared them for publication he said, "I expect they will dazzle the Berlin Philistines like a ray of sunlight."

The next year he lost two of his best friends, Dr. Billroth and Hans von Bülow, which saddened him very much. Despite his estrangement from Billroth he still had hidden within him a deep affection for the surgeon-musician.

As Brahms mourned the loss of his two friends, there suddenly came a letter from Hamburg offering him at last the conductorship of the Philharmonic Orchestra, the position he had desired for so many years. But alas, it had come too late. Brahms wrote to the governing board of the orchestra:

Gentlemen:

There are not many things that I have desired so long and so ardently at the time . . . that is, at the right time. Many years had to pass before I could reconcile myself to the thought of being forced to walk other paths. Had things gone according to my wish, I might today be celebrating my jubilee with you, while you would be, as you are today, looking for a capable younger man. May you find him soon, and may he work in your interests with the same good will, the same modest degree of ability, and the same wholehearted zeal, as would have done

Yours sincerely
J. Brahms

Brahms had neither forgotten nor forgiven Hamburg for neglecting him all these years.

During the summer of 1894 he composed two very beautiful and moving clarinet sonatas, full of a pensiveness and resignation, which were performed the following January at a Brahms Festival in Leipzig. They became the beloved works not only of clarinetists but of all who heard them. Three concerts of his compositions were given in one week, consisting of orchestral works, chamber music, piano concertos, and sonatas. Brahms conducted, and the pianist Eugen d'Albert, whom the composer greatly admired, played two of Brahms's piano concertos in one evening. Some months later there was a music festival in Meiningen which lasted three days. At these concerts only the works of Bach, Beethoven, and Brahms were played. His "Song of Triumph," written to celebrate Germany's victory over France and Bismarck's unification of Germany, a work for eight-part chorus, baritone solo, and orchestra, was performed. Also played were his *First Symphony* and his "Double Concerto."

Visitors came from all over Europe. And in honor of the occasion Brahms appeared in white tie and tails, which he had put on in the morning for the evening performance and reception. When asked why he dressed so early, he said it was too much bother changing later. "If I am compelled to wear tails, I might as well do it right away in the morning so that I won't have to worry about it for the rest of the day."

A few months later, at the Zurich Music Festival, his "Song of Triumph" was performed before Beethoven's *Ninth Symphony*. On the ceiling of the concert hall Brahms saw his portrait painted next to that of Beethoven, Mozart, and other great composers; and although flattered he felt unworthy to be in such company. Robert Schumann's prophecy about him had come true. All kinds of honors were being bestowed on him, and then there came news that he had been left a legacy of $5,000 by an anonymous English admirer. Touched by such a generous bequest he decided to use the entire sum for charitable purposes.

Brahms came to see Clara just before the Zurich Festival, and his warmth and affection reassured her; she saw that he was the same kind, good Johannes and that the harshness he showed at times was not a real part of his fine character. He had sent her his "Third Sonata," composed many years before. She was so enchanted by it that she wrote in her diary,

> *I am currently reveling in Brahms's "Third Sonata," which I have started practicing. . . . To my vast sorrow it is a great strain now for me to play. . . . Ah, how am I ever to live if I should have to give up playing altogether? It is doubly hard for an artist to grow old. I still have all my mental faculties and my finger agility . . . no technical difficulties exist for me. But my nerves have gone. What a bitter trial!*

Several years earlier Clara and Brahms had agreed to return each other's letters and destroy them for fear their loving tone might be misleading to strangers after they were gone. Brahms sent Clara her letters; but when they came she did not destroy all of them. She managed to wheedle out of him a few of his letters to which she was especially attached, and stored

155

them in an old trunk, the key of which she hid. The rest were thrown into the Rhine by Brahms.

No day went by without her practicing, and now that she was no longer giving concerts she took trips with her elder daughters to Switzerland. As the years went on and she became more frail, the days seeming longer without her ability to work, she wondered where she would find the courage to live on. Her daughter Marie remained unmarried, wishing only to look after her mother; Eugenie had gone to live and work in England. It was now Marie who wrote the letters to Brahms for her mother. She had to tell him that her mother was mostly confined to her bed, excepting for short carriage rides on sunny afternoons.

Soon Brahms got word that Clara had had a stroke; alarmed, he immediately canceled an engagement in Merano so that if the news about her grew worse he could go to her at once. He wrote to Joachim about the seriousness of Clara's condition, saying, "When she has gone from us, will not our faces glow with joy whenever we think of her?"

On his birthday in May, Clara, ill as she was, managed to send him a short note of congratulation. Never had she let a birthday of his pass without a letter or a gift. It came a day late, and Brahms wrote to her, "What's last is best! Never have I found this more true than today, with the arrival of the words I deem most precious—yours!"

The days were full of dread and worry as Brahms thought of her imminent loss. It was during this time that he composed the "Four Serious Songs," based on Bible texts concerning death, that were to become Clara's dirge. A few days after his sixty-third birthday, in May 1896, while he was at Ischl, a telegram came to notify him that Clara, seventy-seven, had died peacefully and that the funeral was to be in Bonn. She would lie beside her Robert who had died forty years earlier. In his sorrow and excitement Brahms took the wrong train and had to return and get the right one. And so he missed his beloved friend's funeral. He lamented, "I have lost the friend who was the most beautiful experience of my life, its greatest wealth, and its noblest fulfillment."

The physical and emotional strain of the journey, of standing beside her grave and Robert's in Bonn, had a bad and lasting effect on Brahms. By the time he returned to Ischl he had caught a cold and was so exhausted that he simply could not recover his usual vigor and energy, nor could he resume his usual activities. Friends noticed how sick and yellowish he looked and they begged him to see a doctor. The Ischl doctor thought he had jaundice and advised him to go to the spa in Karlsbad. But a Viennese doctor, called in as a consultant, found that his liver was enlarged; it soon became apparent that Brahms had cancer, the same ailment from which his father had died. Not realizing his serious condition, Brahms went to the spas at Ischl and to Karlsbad for the mineral tonics, hoping the "cures" would benefit him. While there he was visited by loving and anxious friends, among them Dr. Engelmann from Utrecht, who examined him and later sent his son-in-law, an eminent surgeon, to see him in Vienna in case something could still be done for him.

Brahms tried to be as light-hearted and gay as before, refusing to accept his illness as anything but some temporary discomfort. The only work he produced that summer were the eleven choral preludes for organ. One of them was a fantasy on the chorale, "Oh, World, I Must Depart from Thee." Brahms considered these choral preludes to be "little trifles," and although gravely ill he labored on them. The choral melodies woven into these organ works had been sung in church by Brahms during his childhood and were full of delicate spiritual beauty. The last choral prelude of his music was "Before Thy Throne I Now Must Stand." It was the same one with which Bach said farewell to the world.

In the autumn his health was failing so noticeably and he had grown so thin that there was more than ever deep concern for him. When he returned to Vienna he went to a few musical parties, but he was often so weak that he fell asleep. He kept fighting against his illness, unaware of its gravity, and tried to take walks as before; but he soon found it impossible and had instead to accept rides in the carriages of his friends.

He spent Christmas with friends, and the next month, in January 1897, attended a remarkable performance of his "String Quintet in G Major," played by Joachim and his group. When Joachim insisted that Brahms come forward to receive the great applause, Brahms did so most reluctantly; but he was so moved by the way Joachim had played it that he wished to show his appreciation.

In March his *Fourth Symphony,* as well as Dvořák's new cello concerto, was performed by the Vienna Philharmonic Orchestra. Brahms sat hidden in the directors' box of the concert hall, listening intently. The sight of him, so thin and changed, made his friends fearful. The applause after each movement of his symphony was deafening. The audience shouted, waved, wept with emotion. How grateful Brahms was to the warm-hearted Viennese who had made him so welcome!

This was the last time Brahms was to hear a work of his performed. Later in the month he wrote to Joachim, "I am going downhill; every word spoken or written is a strain. Is it a life at all, so solitary? The only true immortality is in children."

Friends showed their loving concern by writing to him, by sending him flowers and gifts, including his favorite Rhine wine. Trying not to worry his stepmother, a few days before his death he wrote her, "I have been lying down a little for a change, so writing is uncomfortable for me. But otherwise do not be alarmed. My condition is unchanged, and, as usual, all I need is patience."

Now Brahms stayed home in the evening and sometimes found the strength to go to the piano to play a little.

On April 3, 1897, just a month before his sixty-fourth birthday, Johannes Brahms died. All the important musical centers of Europe sent representatives to his funeral. The ships lay at anchor in the Hamburg harbor, their flags at half-mast.

There were no close relatives to mourn him, for his parents, sister, and brother had all died before him, and he had never had a wife or children. The funeral torches were carried by his devoted friends, among them Dvořák, for whom he had done so much and who justified his belief in him. Brahms's grave in Vienna was close to those of Beethoven and Schubert, and only a short distance from the monument to Mozart. They would have considered him fit company.

Perhaps, after all, Brahms had been right in not marrying, for he, like Beethoven, belonged to the world and to his noble music which shows his humanity and goodness. The many acts of kindness and generosity which he did secretly and unostentatiously to help people and not make them feel obligated far outweighed his occasional brambliness. He would be remembered not only for his great music but also for his generous heart.